Diane Lindsey Reeves
with Gail Karlitz

An imprint of Infobase Publishing

Career Ideas for Teens in Law and Public Safety

Checkmark Books
An imprint of Infobase Publishing
132 West 31st Street
New York NY 10001

The Library of Congress has cataloged the hardcover edition as follows:

Reeves, Diane Lindsey, 1959-
Career ideas for teens in law and public safety / Diane Lindsey Reeves, with Gail Karlitz.
p. cm.
Includes index.
ISBN 0-8160-5291-3 (hc: alk. paper)
1. Criminal justice, Administration of—Vocational guidance—United States. 2. Law—Vocational guidance—United States. I. Karlitz, Gail. II. Title.
HV9950.R437 2004
363.1'023'73—dc22

2005011063

ISBN: 0-8160-6922-0

Text design by Joel and Sandy Armstrong
Cover design by Nora Wertz
Illustrations by Matt Wood

Printed in the United States of America

VB PKG 10 9 8 7 6 5 4 3 2 1

This book is printed on acid-free paper.

contents

acknowledgments

A million thanks to the people who took the time to share their career stories and provide photos for this book:

Terri Arnold
Robert Glaser
Wayne Polette
Laura Rodriguez
Carrie Stuart Parks
Daniel B. Vasquez

And a big thank-you to the contributing writers who helped fill these pages with important and interesting information:

Christen Brownlee
Carli Entin
Samantha Henderson

career ideas for teens

welcome to your future

Q: What's one of the most boring questions adults ask teens?

A: "So . . . what do you want to be when you grow up?"

Well-meaning adults always seem so interested in what you plan to be.

You, on the other hand, are just trying to make it through high school in one piece.

But you may still have a nagging feeling that you really need to find some direction and think about what you want to do with your life.

When it comes to choosing your life's work there's some good news and some bad news. The good news is that, according to the U.S. Bureau of Labor Statistics, you have more than 12,000 different occupations to choose from. With that many options there's got to be something that's just right for you.

Right?

Absolutely.

But . . .

Here comes the bad news.

THERE ARE MORE THAN 12,000 DIFFERENT OCCUPATIONS TO CHOOSE FROM!

How in the world are you ever going to figure out which one is right for you?

We're so glad you asked!

Helping high school students like you make informed choices about their future is what this book (and each of the other titles in the *Career Ideas for Teens* series) is all about. Here you'll encounter 10 tough questions designed to help you answer the biggest one of all: "What in the world am I going to do after I graduate from high school?"

The *Career Ideas for Teens* series enables you to expand your horizons beyond the "doctor, teacher, lawyer" responses common to those new to the career exploration process. The books provide a no-pressure introduction to real jobs that real people do. And they offer a chance to "try on" different career options before committing to a specific college program or career path. Each title in this series is based on one of the 16 career clusters established by the U.S. Department of Education.

And what is a career cluster, you ask? Career clusters are based on a simple and very useful concept. Each cluster consists of all entry-level through professional-level occupations in a broad industry area. All of the jobs and industries in a cluster have many things in common. This organizational structure makes it easier for people like you to get a handle on the big world of work. So instead of rushing headlong into a mind-boggling exploration of the entire universe of career opportunities, you get a chance to tiptoe into smaller, more manageable segments first.

We've used this career cluster concept to organize the *Career Ideas for Teens* series of books. For example, careers related to the arts, communication, and entertainment are organized or "clustered" into the *Career Ideas for Teens in the Arts and Communications* title; a wide variety of health care professions are included in *Career Ideas for Teens in Health Science*; and so on.

Clueless as to what some of these industries are all about? Can't even imagine how something like manufacturing or public administration could possibly relate to you?

No problem.

You're about to find out. Just be prepared to expect the unexpected as you venture out into the world of work. There are some pretty incredible options out there, and some pretty surprising ones too. In fact, it's quite possible that you'll discover that the ideal career for you is one you had never heard of before.

Whatever you do, don't cut yourself short by limiting yourself to just one book in the series. You may find that your initial interests guide you towards the health sciences field—which would, of course, be a good place to start. However, you may discover some new "twists" with a look through the arts and communications book. There you may find a way to blend your medical interests with your exceptional writing and speaking skills by considering becoming a public relations (PR) specialist for a hospital or pharmaceutical company. Or look at the book on education to see about becoming a public health educator or school nurse.

Before you get started, you should know that this book is divided into three sections, each representing an important step toward figuring out what to do with your life.

The first titles in the *Career Ideas for Teens* series focus on:

- Arts and Communications
- Education and Training
- Health Science
- Information Technology
- Law and Public Safety

Before You Get Started

Unlike most books, this one is meant to be actively experienced, rather than merely read. Passive perusal won't cut it. Energetic engagement is what it takes to figure out something as important as the rest of your life.

As we've already mentioned, you'll encounter 10 important questions as you work your way through this book. Following each Big Question is an activity designated with a symbol that looks like this:

Every time you see this symbol, you'll know it's time to invest a little energy in your future by getting out your notebook or binder, a pen or pencil, and doing whatever the instructions direct you to do. If this book is your personal property, you can choose to do the activities right in the book. But you still might want to make copies of your finished products to go in a binder so they are all in one place for easy reference.

When you've completed all the activities, you'll have your own personal **Big Question AnswerBook**, a planning guide representing a straightforward and truly effective process you can use throughout your life to make fully informed career decisions.

discover you at work

This first section focuses on a very important subject: You. It poses four Big Questions that are designed specifically to help you "discover you":

- Big Question #1: **who are you?**
- Big Question #2: **what are your interests and strengths?**
- Big Question #3: **what are your work values?**

Then, using an interest assessment tool developed by the U.S. Department of Labor and implemented with your very vivid imagination, you'll picture yourself doing some of the things that people actually do for their jobs. In other words, you'll start "discovering you at work" by answering the following:

- Big Question #4: **what's your work personality?**

Unfortunately, this first step is often a misstep for many people. Or make that a "missed" step. When you talk with the adults in your life about their career choices, you're likely to find that some of them never even considered the idea of choosing a career based on personal preferences and strengths. You're also likely to learn that if they had it to do over again, this step would definitely play a significant role in the choices they would make.

explore your options

There's more than meets the eye when it comes to finding the best career to pursue. There are also countless ways to blend talent or passion in these areas in some rather unexpected and exciting ways. Get ready to find answers to two more Big Questions as you browse through an entire section of career profiles:

? Big Question #5: **do you have the right skills?**
? Big Question #6: **are you on the right path?**

experiment with success

At long last you're ready to give this thing called career planning a trial run. Here's where you'll encounter three Big Questions that will unleash critical decision-making strategies and skills that will serve you well throughout a lifetime of career success.

While you're at it, take some time to sit in on a roundtable discussion with successful professionals representing a very impressive array of careers related to this industry. Many of their experiences will apply to your own life, even if you don't plan to pursue the same careers.

? Big Question #7: **who knows what you need to know?**
? Big Question #8: **how can you find out what a career is really like?**
? Big Question #9: **how do you know when you've made the right choice?**

Then as you begin to pull all your new insights and ideas together, you'll come to one final question:

? Big Question #10: **what's next?**

As you get ready to take the plunge, remember that this is a book about possibilities and potential. You can use it to make the most of your future work!

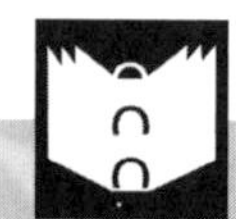

Here's what you'll need to complete the Big Question AnswerBook:

- A notebook or binder for the completed activities included in all three sections of the book
- An openness to new ideas
- Complete and completely candid answers to the 10 Big Question activities

So don't just read it, do it.
Plan it.
Dream it.

SECTION 1 discover you at work

The goal here is to get some clues about who you are and what you should do with your life. As time goes by, you will grow older, become more educated, and have more experiences, but many things that truly define you are not likely to change. Even now you possess very strong characteristics—genuine qualities that mark you as the unique and gifted person that you undoubtedly are.

It's impossible to overestimate the importance of giving your wholehearted attention to this step. You, after all, are the most valuable commodity you'll ever have to offer a future employer. Finding work that makes the most of your assets often means the difference between enjoying a rewarding career and simply earning a paycheck.

You've probably already experienced the satisfaction of a good day's work. You know what we mean—those days when you get all your assignments in on time, you're prepared for the pop quiz your teacher sprung on you, and you beat your best time during sports practice. You may be exhausted at the end of the day but you can't help but feel good about yourself and your accomplishments. A well-chosen career can provide that same sense of satisfaction. Since you're likely to spend upwards of 40 years doing some kind of work, well-informed choices make a lot of sense!

Let's take a little time for you to understand yourself and connect what you discover about yourself to the world of work.

To find a career path that's right for you, we'll tackle these three Big Questions first:

- **who are you?**
- **what are your interests and strengths?**
- **what are your work values?**

Big Question #1: **who are you?**

Have you ever noticed how quickly new students in your school or new families in your community find the people who are most like them? If you've ever been the "new" person yourself, you've probably spent your first few days sizing up the general population and then getting in with the people who dress in clothes a lot like yours, appreciate the same style of music, or maybe even root for the same sports teams.

Given that this process happens so naturally—if not necessarily on purpose—it should come as no surprise that many people lean toward jobs that surround them with people most like them. When people with common interests, common values, and complementary talents come together in the workplace, the results can be quite remarkable.

Many career aptitude tests, including the one developed by the U.S. Department of Labor and included later in this book, are based on the theory that certain types of people do better at certain types of jobs. It's like a really sophisticated matchmaking service. Take your basic strengths and interests and match them to the strengths and interests required by specific occupations.

It makes sense when you think about it. When you want to find a career that's ideally suited for you, find out what people like you are doing and head off in that direction!

There's just one little catch.

The only way to recognize other people like you is to recognize yourself. Who are you anyway? What are you like? What's your basic approach to life and work?

Now's as good a time as any to find out. Let's start by looking at who you are in a systematic way. This process will ultimately help you understand how to identify personally appropriate career options.

Big Activity #1:

who are you?

On a sheet of paper, if this book doesn't belong to you, create a list of adjectives that best describe you. You should be able to come up with at least 15 qualities that apply to you. There's no need to make judgments about whether these qualities are good or bad. They just are. They represent who you are and can help you understand what you bring to the workforce.

(If you get stuck, ask a trusted friend or adult to help describe especially strong traits they see in you.)

Some of the types of qualities you may choose to include are:

- **How you relate to others:**
  Are you shy? Outgoing? Helpful? Dependent? Empathic? In charge? Agreeable? Challenging? Persuasive? Popular? Impatient? A loner?
- **How you approach new situations:**
  Are you adventurous? Traditional? Cautious? Enthusiastic? Curious?
- **How you feel about change—planned or unplanned:**
  Are you resistant? Adaptable? Flexible? Predictable?
- **How you approach problems:**
  Are you persistent? Spontaneous? Methodical? Creative?
- **How you make decisions:**
  Are you intuitive? Logical? Emotional? Practical? Systematic? Analytical?
- **How you approach life:**
  Are you laid back? Ambitious? Perfectionist? Idealistic? Optimistic? Pessimistic? Self-sufficient?

Feel free to use any of these words if they happen to describe you well, but please don't limit yourself to this list. Pick the best adjectives that paint an accurate picture of the real you. Get more ideas from a dictionary or thesaurus if you'd like.

When you're finished, put the completed list in your Big Question AnswerBook.

Big Activity #1: **who are you?**

fifteen qualities that describe me		
1	2	3
4	5	6
7	8	9
10	11	12
13	14	15
etc.		

Big Question #2: what are your interests and strengths?

For many people, doing something they like to do is the most important part of deciding on a career path—even more important than how much money they can earn!

We don't all like to do the same things—and that's good. For some people, the ideal vacation is lying on a beach, doing absolutely nothing; others would love to spend weeks visiting museums and historic places. Some people wish they had time to learn to skydive or fly a plane; others like to learn to cook gourmet meals or do advanced math.

If we all liked the same things, the world just wouldn't work very well. There would be incredible crowds in some places and ghost towns in others. Some of our natural resources would be overburdened; others would never be used. We would all want to eat at the same restaurant, wear the same outfit, see the same movie, and live in the same place. How boring!

So let's get down to figuring out what you most like to do and how you can spend your working life doing just that. In some ways your answer to this question is all you really need to know about choosing a career, because the people who enjoy their work the most are those who do something they enjoy. We're not talking rocket science here. Just plain old common sense.

Big Activity # 2:

what are your interests and strengths?

Imagine this: No school, no job, no homework, no chores, no obligations at all. All the time in the world you want to do all the things you like most. You know what we're talking about—those things that completely grab your interest and keep you engrossed for hours without your getting bored. Those kinds of things you do really well—sometimes effortlessly, sometimes with extraordinary (and practiced) skill.

And, by the way, EVERYONE has plenty of both interests and strengths. Some are just more visible than others.

Step 1: Write the three things you most enjoy doing on a sheet of paper, if this book doesn't belong to you. Leave lots of space after each thing.

Step 2: Think about some of the deeper reasons why you enjoy each of these activities—the motivations beyond "it's fun." Do you enjoy shopping because it gives you a chance to be with your friends? Because it allows you to find new ways to express your individuality? Because you enjoy the challenge of finding bargains or things no one else has discovered? Or because it's fun to imagine the lifestyle you'll be able to lead when you're finally rich and famous? In the blank spaces, record the reasons why you enjoy each activity.

Step 3: Keep this list handy in your Big Question AnswerBook so that you can refer to it any time you have to make a vocational decision. Sure, you may have to update the list from time to time as your interests change. But one thing is certain. The kind of work you'll most enjoy will be linked in some way to the activities on that list. Count on it.

Maybe one of your favorite things to do is "play basketball." Does that mean the only way you'll ever be happy at work is to play professional basketball?

Maybe.

Maybe not.

Use your *why* responses to read between the lines. The *whys* can prove even more important than the *whats*. Perhaps what you like most about playing basketball is the challenge or the chance to be part of a team that shares a common goal. Maybe you really like pushing yourself to improve. Or it could be the rush associated with competition and the thrill of winning.

The more you uncover your own *whys*, the closer you'll be to discovering important clues about the kinds of work that are best for you.

Big Activity #2: **what are your interests and strengths?**

things you enjoy doing	why you enjoy doing them
1	• • •
2	• • •
3	• • •

Big Question #3: what are your work values?

Chances are, you've never given a moment's thought to this next question. At least not in the context of career planning.

You already looked at who you are and what you enjoy and do well. The idea being, of course, to seek out career options that make the most of your innate qualities, preferences, and natural abilities.

As you start checking into various careers, you'll discover one more dimension associated with making personally appropriate career choices. You'll find that even though people may have the exact same job title, they may execute their jobs in dramatically different ways. For instance, everyone knows about teachers. They teach things to other people. Period.

But wait. If you line up 10 aspiring teachers in one room, you may be surprised to discover how vastly different their interpretations of the job may be. There are the obvious differences, of course. One may want to teach young children; one may want to teach adults. One will focus on teaching math, while another one focuses on teaching Spanish.

Look a little closer and you'll find even greater disparity in the choices they make. One may opt for the prestige (and paycheck) of working in an Ivy League college, while another is completely committed to teaching disadvantaged children in a remote area of the Appalachian Mountains. One may approach teaching simply as a way to make a living, while another devotes almost every waking hour to working with his or her students.

These subtle but significant differences reflect what's truly important to each person. In a word, they reflect the person's values—those things that are most important to them.

People's values depend on many factors—their upbringing, their life experiences, their goals and ambitions, their religious beliefs, and, quite frankly, the way they view the world and their role in it. Very few people share exactly the same values. However, that doesn't necessarily mean that some people are right and others are wrong. It just means they have different perspectives.

Here's a story that shows how different values can be reflected in career choices.

Imagine: It's five years after college graduation and a group of college friends are back together for the first time. They catch up about their lives, their families, and their careers. Listen in on one of their reunion conversations and see if you can guess what each is doing now.

Alice: I have the best career. Every day I get the chance to help kids with special needs get a good education.

Bob: I love my career, too. It's great to know that I am making my town a safer place for everyone.

Cathy: It was tough for me to commit to more school after college. But I'm glad I did. After all I went through when my parents divorced, I'm glad I can be there to make things easier for other families.

David: I know how you feel. I'm glad I get to do something that helps companies function smoothly and keep our economy strong. Of course, you remember that I had a hard time deciding whether to pursue this career or teaching! This way I get the best of both worlds.

Elizabeth: It's great that we both ended up in the corporate world. You know that I was always intrigued by the stock market.

So exactly what is each of the five former freshman friends doing today? Have you made your guesses?

Alice is a lawyer. She specializes in education law. She makes sure that school districts provide special needs children with all of the resources they are entitled to under the law.

Bob is a lawyer. He is a prosecuting attorney and makes his town safer by ensuring that justice is served when someone commits a crime.

Cathy is a lawyer. She practices family law. She helps families negotiate separation and divorce agreements and makes sure that adoption and custody proceedings protect everyone involved. Sometimes she even provides legal intervention to protect adults or children who are in abusive situations.

David is a lawyer. He practices employment law. He helps companies set up policies that follow fair employment practices. He also gives seminars to managers, teaching them what the law says and means about sexual harassment, discrimination, and termination of employment.

Elizabeth is a lawyer. She practices corporate law and is indispensable to corporations with legal responsibilities towards stockholders and the government.

Wow! All five friends have the same job title. But each describes his/her job so differently! All five were able to enter the field of law and focus on the things that are most important to them: quality education, freedom from crime, protection of families and children, fairness in the workplace, and corporate economic growth. Identifying and honoring your personal values is an important part of choosing your life's work.

Big Activity #3:
what are your work values?

Step 1: Look at the following chart. If this book doesn't belong to you, divide a sheet of paper into the following three columns:

- **Essential**
  Statements that fall into this column are very important to you. If the job doesn't satisfy these needs, you're not interested.
- **Okay**
  Great if the job satisfies these needs, but you can also live without them.
- **No Way**
  Statements that fall into this column represent needs that are not at all important to you or things you'd rather do without or simply couldn't tolerate.

Step 2: Look over the following list of statements representing different work values. Rewrite each statement in the appropriate column. Does the first statement represent something that is critical to you to have in your work? If so, write it in the first column. No big deal either way? Write it in the second column. Couldn't stand it? Write it in the third column. Repeat the same process for each of the value statements.

Step 3: When you're finished, place your complete work values chart in your Big Question AnswerBook.

Got it? Then get with it.

Really think about these issues. Lay it on the line. What values are so deeply ingrained in you that you'd be absolutely miserable if you had to sacrifice them for a job? Religious beliefs and political leanings fall into this category for some people.

Which ones provide room for some give and take? Things like vacation and benefits, working hours, and other issues along those lines may be completely negotiable for some people, but absolutely not for others.

Just remember, wherever you go and whatever you do, be sure that the choices you make are true to you.

Big Activity #3: **what are your work values?**

work values	essential	okay	no way
1. I can count on plenty of opportunity for advancement and taking on more responsibility.			
2. I can work to my fullest potential using all of my abilities.			
3. I would be able to give directions and instructions to others.			
4. I would always know exactly what my manager expects of me.			
5. I could structure my own day.			
6. I would be very busy all day.			
7. I would work in attractive and pleasant surroundings.			
8. My coworkers would be people I might choose as friends.			
9. I would get frequent feedback about my performance.			
10. I could continue my education to progress to an even higher level job.			
11. Most of the time I would be able to work alone.			
12. I would know precisely what I need to do to succeed at the job.			
13. I could make decisions on my own.			

Big Activity #3: **what are your work values?**

work values	essential	okay	no way
14. I would have more than the usual amount of vacation time.			
15. I would be working doing something I really believe in.			
16. I would feel like part of a team.			
17. I would find good job security and stable employment opportunities in the industry.			
18. I could depend on my manager for the training I need.			
19. I would earn lots of money.			
20. I would feel a sense of accomplishment in my work.			
21. I would be helping other people.			
22. I could try out my own ideas.			
23. I would not need to have further training or education to do this job.			
24. I would get to travel a lot.			
25. I could work the kind of hours I need to balance work, family, and personal responsibilities.	ESSENTIAL	OKAY	NO WAY

To summarize in my own words, the work values most important to me include:

Big Question #4: what is your work personality?

Congratulations. After completing the first three activities, you've already discovered a set of skills you can use throughout your life. Basing key career decisions on factors associated with who you are, what you enjoy and do well, and what's most important about work will help you today as you're just beginning to explore the possibilities, as well as into the future as you look for ways to cultivate your career.

Now that you've got that mastered, let's move on to another important skill. This one blends some of what you just learned about yourself with what you need to learn about the real world of work. It's a reality check of sorts as you align and merge your personal interests and abilities with those required in different work situations. At the end of this task you will identify your personal interest profile.

This activity is based on the work of Dr. John Holland. Dr. Holland conducted groundbreaking research that identified different characteristics in people. He found that he could classify people into six basic groups based on which characteristics tended to occur at the same time. He also found that the characteristics that defined the different groups of people were also characteristics that corresponded to success in different groups of occupations. The result of all that work was a classification system that identifies and names six distinct groups of people who share personal interests or characteristics and are likely to be successful in a group of clearly identified jobs.

Dr. Holland's work is respected by workforce professionals everywhere and is widely used by employers and employment agencies to help people get a handle on the best types of work to pursue.

The following Work Interest Profiler (WIP) is based on Dr. Holland's theories and was developed by the U.S. Department of Labor's Employment and Training Administration as part of an important project called O*Net. O*Net is a system used in all 50 states to provide career and employment services to thousands of people every year. It's a system you'll want to know about when it's time to take that first plunge into the world of work. If you'd like, you can find more information about this system at ***http://online.onetcenter.org***.

Big Activity #4:

what is your work personality?

By completing O*Net's Work Interest Profiler (WIP), you'll gain valuable insight into the types of work that are right for you.

here's how it works

The WIP lists many activities that real people do at real jobs. Your task is to read a brief statement about each of these activities and decide if it is something you think you'd enjoy doing. Piece of cake!

Don't worry about whether you have enough education or training to perform the activity. And, for now, forget about how much money you would make performing the activity.

Just boil it down to whether or not you'd like performing each work activity. If you'd like it, put a check in the *like* column that corresponds to each of the six interest areas featured in the test on the handy dandy chart you're about to create (or use the one in the book if it's yours). If you don't like it, put that check in the *dislike* column. What if you don't have a strong opinion on a particular activity? That's okay. Count that one as *unsure*.

Be completely honest with yourself. No one else is going to see your chart. If you check things you think you "should" check, you are not helping yourself find the career that will make you happy.

Before you start, create a chart for yourself. Your scoring sheet will have six horizontal rows and three vertical columns. Label the six rows as Sections 1 through 6, and label the three columns *like*, *dislike*, and *unsure*.

how to complete the Work Interest Profiler

Step 1: Start with Section 1.

Step 2: Look at the first activity and decide whether you would like to do it as part of your job.

Step 3: Put a mark in the appropriate column (*Like*, *Dislike*, or *Unsure*) on the Section 1 row.

Step 4: Continue for every activity in Section 1. Then do Sections 2 through 6.

Step 5: When you've finished all of the sections, count the number of marks you have in each column and write down the total.

Remember, this is not a test! There are no right or wrong answers. You are completing this profile to learn more about yourself and your work-related interests.

Also, once you've completed this activity, be sure to put your chart and any notes in your Big Question AnswerBook.

Ready? Let's go!

Section 1

1. Drive a taxi
2. Repair household appliances
3. Catch fish as a member of a fishing crew
4. Paint houses
5. Assemble products in a factory
6. Install flooring in houses
7. Perform lawn care services
8. Drive a truck to deliver packages to homes and offices
9. Work on an offshore oil-drilling rig
10. Put out forest fires
11. Fix a broken faucet
12. Refinish furniture
13. Guard money in an armored car
14. Lay brick or tile
15. Operate a dairy farm
16. Raise fish in a fish hatchery
17. Build a brick walkway
18. Enforce fish and game laws
19. Assemble electronic parts
20. Build kitchen cabinets
21. Maintain the grounds of a park
22. Operate a motorboat to carry passengers
23. Set up and operate machines to make products
24. Spray trees to prevent the spread of harmful insects
25. Monitor a machine on an assembly line

Section 2

1. Study space travel
2. Develop a new medicine
3. Study the history of past civilizations
4. Develop a way to better predict the weather
5. Determine the infection rate of a new disease
6. Study the personalities of world leaders
7. Investigate the cause of a fire
8. Develop psychological profiles of criminals
9. Study whales and other types of marine life
10. Examine blood samples using a microscope
11. Invent a replacement for sugar
12. Study genetics
13. Do research on plants or animals
14. Study weather conditions
15. Investigate crimes
16. Study ways to reduce water pollution
17. Develop a new medical treatment or procedure
18. Diagnose and treat sick animals
19. Conduct chemical experiments
20. Study rocks and minerals
21. Do laboratory tests to identify diseases
22. Study the structure of the human body
23. Plan a research study
24. Study the population growth of a city
25. Make a map of the bottom of the ocean

Section 3

1. Paint sets for a play
2. Create special effects for movies
3. Write reviews of books or movies
4. Compose or arrange music
5. Design artwork for magazines
6. Pose for a photographer
7. Create dance routines for a show
8. Play a musical instrument
9. Edit movies
10. Sing professionally
11. Announce a radio show
12. Perform stunts for a movie or television show
13. Design sets for plays
14. Act in a play
15. Write a song
16. Perform jazz or tap dance
17. Sing in a band
18. Direct a movie
19. Write scripts for movies or television shows
20. Audition singers and musicians for a musical show
21. Conduct a musical choir
22. Perform comedy routines in front of an audience
23. Dance in a Broadway show
24. Perform as an extra in movies, plays, or television shows
25. Write books or plays

Section 4

1. Teach children how to play sports
2. Help people with family-related problems
3. Teach an individual an exercise routine
4. Perform nursing duties in a hospital
5. Help people with personal or emotional problems
6. Teach work and living skills to people with disabilities
7. Assist doctors in treating patients
8. Work with juveniles on probation
9. Supervise the activities of children at a camp
10. Teach an elementary school class
11. Perform rehabilitation therapy
12. Help elderly people with their daily activities
13. Help people who have problems with drugs or alcohol
14. Teach a high school class
15. Give career guidance to people
16. Do volunteer work at a non-profit organization
17. Help families care for ill relatives
18. Teach sign language to people with hearing disabilities
19. Help people with disabilities improve their daily living skills
20. Help conduct a group therapy session
21. Work with children with mental disabilities
22. Give CPR to someone who has stopped breathing
23. Provide massage therapy to people
24. Plan exercises for patients with disabilities
25. Counsel people who have a life-threatening illness

Section 5

1. Sell CDs and tapes at a music store
2. Manage a clothing store
3. Sell houses
4. Sell computer equipment in a store
5. Operate a beauty salon or barber shop
6. Sell automobiles
7. Represent a client in a lawsuit
8. Negotiate business contracts
9. Sell a soft drink product line to stores and restaurants
10. Start your own business
11. Be responsible for the operations of a company
12. Give a presentation about a product you are selling
13. Buy and sell land
14. Sell restaurant franchises to individuals
15. Manage the operations of a hotel
16. Negotiate contracts for professional athletes
17. Sell merchandise at a department store
18. Market a new line of clothing
19. Buy and sell stocks and bonds
20. Sell merchandise over the telephone
21. Run a toy store
22. Sell hair-care products to stores and salons
23. Sell refreshments at a movie theater
24. Manage a retail store
25. Sell telephone and other communication equipment

Section 6

1. Develop an office filing system
2. Generate the monthly payroll checks for an office
3. Proofread records or forms
4. Schedule business conferences
5. Enter information into a database
6. Photocopy letters and reports
7. Keep inventory records
8. Record information from customers applying for charge accounts
9. Load computer software into a large computer network
10. Use a computer program to generate customer bills
11. Develop a spreadsheet using computer software
12. Operate a calculator
13. Direct or transfer office phone calls
14. Use a word processor to edit and format documents
15. Transfer funds between banks, using a computer
16. Compute and record statistical and other numerical data
17. Stamp, sort, and distribute office mail
18. Maintain employee records
19. Record rent payments
20. Keep shipping and receiving records
21. Keep accounts payable/receivable for an office
22. Type labels for envelopes and packages
23. Calculate the wages of employees
24. Take notes during a meeting
25. Keep financial records

Section 1
Realistic

	Like	Dislike	Unsure
1.			
2.			
3.			
4.			
5.			
6.			
7.			
8.			
9.			
10.			
11.			
12.			
13.			
14.			
15.			
16.			
17.			
18.			
19.			
20.			
21.			
22.			
23.			
24.			
25.			

Total Realistic

Section 2
Investigative

	Like	Dislike	Unsure
1.			
2.			
3.			
4.			
5.			
6.			
7.			
8.			
9.			
10.			
11.			
12.			
13.			
14.			
15.			
16.			
17.			
18.			
19.			
20.			
21.			
22.			
23.			
24.			
25.			

Total Investigative

Section 3
Artistic

	Like	Dislike	Unsure
1.			
2.			
3.			
4.			
5.			
6.			
7.			
8.			
9.			
10.			
11.			
12.			
13.			
14.			
15.			
16.			
17.			
18.			
19.			
20.			
21.			
22.			
23.			
24.			
25.			

Total Artistic

Section 4
Social

	Like	Dislike	Unsure
1.			
2.			
3.			
4.			
5.			
6.			
7.			
8.			
9.			
10.			
11.			
12.			
13.			
14.			
15.			
16.			
17.			
18.			
19.			
20.			
21.			
22.			
23.			
24.			
25.			

Total Social

Section 5
Enterprising

	Like	Dislike	Unsure
1.			
2.			
3.			
4.			
5.			
6.			
7.			
8.			
9.			
10.			
11.			
12.			
13.			
14.			
15.			
16.			
17.			
18.			
19.			
20.			
21.			
22.			
23.			
24.			
25.			

Total Enterprising

Section 6
Conventional

	Like	Dislike	Unsure
1.			
2.			
3.			
4.			
5.			
6.			
7.			
8.			
9.			
10.			
11.			
12.			
13.			
14.			
15.			
16.			
17.			
18.			
19.			
20.			
21.			
22.			
23.			
24.			
25.			

Total Conventional

What are your top three work personalities? List them here if this is your own book or on a separate piece of paper if it's not.

1. ____________
2. ____________
3. ____________

all done? let's see what it means

Be sure you count up the number of marks in each column on your scoring sheet and write down the total for each column. You will probably notice that you have a lot of *like*s for some sections, and a lot of *dislike*s for other sections. The section that has the most *like*s is your primary interest area. The section with the next highest number of *like*s is your second interest area. The next highest is your third interest area.

Now that you know your top three interest areas, what does it mean about your work personality type? We'll get to that in a minute, but first we are going to answer a couple of other questions that might have crossed your mind:

- What is the best work personality to have?
- What does my work personality mean?

First of all, there is no "best" personality in general. There is, however, a "best" personality for each of us. It's who we really are and how we feel most comfortable. There may be several "best" work personalities for any job because different people may approach the job in different ways. But there is no "best work personality."

Asking about the "best work personality" is like asking whether the "best" vehicle is a sports car, a sedan, a station wagon, or a sports utility vehicle. It all depends on who you are and what you need.

One thing we do know is that our society needs all of the work personalities in order to function effectively. Fortunately, we usually seem to have a good mix of each type.

So, while many people may find science totally boring, there are many other people who find it fun and exciting. Those are the people who invent new technologies, who become doctors and researchers, and who turn natural resources into the things we use every day. Many people may think that spending a day with young children is unbearable, but those who love that environment are the teachers, community leaders, and museum workers that nurture children's minds and personalities.

When everything is in balance, there's a job for every person and a person for every job.

Now we'll get to your work personality. Following are descriptions of each of Dr. Holland's six work personalities that correspond to the six sections in your last exercise. You, like most people, are a unique combination of more than one. A little of this, a lot of that. That's what makes us interesting.

Identify your top three work personalities. Also, pull out your responses to the first three exercises we did. As you read about your top three work personalities, see how they are similar to the way you described yourself earlier.

Type 1
Realistic

Realistic people are often seen as the "Doers." They have mechanical or athletic ability and enjoy working outdoors.

Realistic people like work activities that include practical, hands-on problems and solutions. They enjoy dealing with plants, animals, and real-life materials like wood, tools, and machinery.

Careers that involve a lot of paperwork or working closely with others are usually not attractive to realistic people.

Who you are:
independent
reserved
practical
mechanical
athletic
persistent

What you like to do/what you do well:
build things
train animals
play a sport
fix things
garden
hunt or fish
woodworking
repair cars
refinish furniture

Career possibilities:
aerospace engineer
aircraft pilot
animal breeder
architect
baker/chef
building inspector
carpenter
chemical engineer
civil engineer
construction manager
dental assistant
detective
glazier
jeweler
machinist
oceanographer
optician
park ranger
plumber
police officer
practical nurse
private investigator
radiologist
sculptor

Type 2
Investigative

Investigative people are often seen as the "Thinkers." They much prefer searching for facts and figuring out problems mentally to doing physical activity or leading other people.

If Investigative is one of your strong interest areas, your answers to the earlier exercises probably matched some of these:

Who you are:
curious
logical
independent
analytical
observant
inquisitive

What you like to do/what you do well:
think abstractly
solve problems
use a microscope
do research
fly a plane
explore new subjects
study astronomy
do puzzles
work with a computer

Career possibilities:

aerospace engineer
archaeologist
CAD technician
chemist
chiropractor
computer programmer
coroner
dentist
electrician
ecologist
geneticist
hazardous waste technician
historian
horticulturist
management consultant
medical technologist
meteorologist
nurse practitioner
pediatrician
pharmacist
political scientist
psychologist
software engineer
surgeon
technical writer
veterinarian
zoologist

Type 3
Artistic

Artistic people are the "Creators." People with this primary interest like work activities that deal with the artistic side of things.

Artistic people need to have the opportunity for self-expression in their work. They want to be able to use their imaginations and prefer to work in less structured environments, without clear sets of rules about how things should be done.

Who you are:

imaginative
intuitive
expressive
emotional
creative
independent

What you like to do/what you do well:

draw
paint
play an instrument
visit museums
act
design clothes or rooms
read fiction
travel
write stories, poetry, or music

Career possibilities:

architect
actor
animator
art director
cartoonist
choreographer
costume designer
composer
copywriter
dancer
disc jockey
drama teacher
emcee
fashion designer
graphic designer
illustrator
interior designer
journalist
landscape architect
medical illustrator
photographer
producer
scriptwriter
set designer

Type 4
Social

Social people are known as the "Helpers." They are interested in work that can assist others and promote learning and personal development.

Communication with other people is very important to those in the Social group. They usually do not enjoy jobs that require a great amount of work with objects, machines, or data. Social people like to teach, give advice, help, cure, or otherwise be of service to people.

Who you are:
friendly
outgoing
empathic
persuasive
idealistic
generous

What you like to do/what you do well:
teach others
work in groups
play team sports
care for children
go to parties
help or advise others
meet new people
express yourself
join clubs or organizations

Career possibilities:
animal trainer
arbitrator
art teacher
art therapist
audiologist
child care worker
clergy person
coach
counselor/therapist
cruise director
dental hygienist
employment interviewer
EMT worker
fitness trainer
flight attendant
occupational therapist
police officer
recreational therapist
registered nurse
school psychologist
social worker
substance abuse counselor
teacher
tour guide

Type 5
Enterprising

Enterprising work personalities can be called the "Persuaders." These people like work activities that have to do with starting up and carrying out projects, especially business ventures. They like taking risks for profit, enjoy being responsible for making decisions, and generally prefer action to thought or analysis.

People in the Enterprising group like to work with other people. While the Social group focuses on helping other people, members of the Enterprising group are able to lead, manage, or persuade other people to accomplish the goals of the organization.

Who you are:
assertive
self-confident
ambitious
extroverted
optimistic
adventurous

What you like to do/what you do well:
organize activities
sell things
promote ideas

discuss politics
hold office in clubs
give talks or speeches
meet people
initiate projects
start your own business

Career possibilities:
advertising
chef
coach, scout
criminal investigator
economist
editor
foreign service officer
funeral director
hotel manager
journalist
lawyer
lobbyist
public relations specialist
newscaster
restaurant manager
sales manager
school principal
ship's captain
stockbroker
umpire, referee
urban planner

Type 6 Conventional

People in the Conventional group are the "Organizers." They like work activities that follow set procedures and routines. They are more comfortable and proficient working with data and detail than they are with generalized ideas.

Conventional people are happiest in work situations where the lines of authority are clear, where they know exactly what responsibilities are expected of them, and where there are precise standards for the work.

Who you are:
well-organized
accurate
practical
persistent
conscientious
ambitious

What you like to do/what you do well:
work with numbers
type accurately
collect or organize things
follow up on tasks
be punctual
be responsible for details
proofread
keep accurate records
understand regulations

Career possibilities:
accountant
actuary
air traffic controller
assessor
budget analyst
building inspector
chief financial officer
corporate treasurer
cost estimator
court reporter
economist
environmental compliance lawyer
fire inspector
insurance underwriter
legal secretary
mathematician
medical secretary
proofreader
tax preparer

law and public safety careers work personality chart

Once you've discovered your own unique work personality code, you can use it to explore the careers profiled in this book and elsewhere. Do keep in mind though that this code is just a tool meant to help focus your search. It's not meant to box you in or to keep you from pursuing any career that happens to capture your imagination.

Following is a chart listing the work personality codes associated with each of the careers profiled in this book.

	Realistic	Investigative	Artistic	Social	Enterprising	Conventional
My Work Personality Code (mark your top three areas)						
Administrative Law Judge		X		X	X	X
Arbitrator and Mediator		X		X	X	X
Bailiff				X	X	X
Border Patrol Agent	X	X			X	X
Coroner	X	X				X
Correctional Officer	X			X		X
Court Reporter				X	X	X
Emergency Management Specialist		X		X	X	
Emergency Medical Technician	X	X			X	
Federal Special Agent		X		X	X	
Fire Investigator	X			X	X	
Fire Marshal	X	X		X		X
Forensic Artist	X		X	X		
Forensic Nurse	X	X	X	X		
Forensic Pathologist	X	X				X
Forensic Science Technician	X	X				X

	Realistic	Investigative	Artistic	Social	Enterprising	Conventional
Hazardous Materials Technician	X	X			X	
Humane Law Enforcement Officer	X	X		X		
Immigration Officer	X	X			X	X
Information Systems Security Specialist	X	X				X
Insurance Investigator	X			X	X	
Judge				X	X	X
Lawyer		X		X	X	X
Legal Nurse Consultant		X		X		X
Municipal Firefighter	X			X	X	
Occupational Health and Safety Specialist	X			X	X	
Paralegal				X	X	X
Parole and Probation Officer	X			X	X	X
Police Officer		X		X	X	
Private Investigator	X			X	X	
Public Safety Dispatcher				X	X	X
Public Safety Diver	X				X	
Recreational Services Safety Specialist	X				X	
Wildland Firefighter	X			X	X	
Wildlife Conservation Officer	X	X			X	

Now it's time to move on to the next big step in the Big Question process. While the first steps focused on you, the next one focuses on the world of work. It includes profiles of a wide variety of occupations related to law and public safety, suggested resources for fully exploring each option, hands-on activities for getting a sense of what each career is really like, and a mind-boggling list of other careers to consider when wanting to blend passion or talent in these areas with your life's work.

explore your options

By now, you probably have a fairly good understanding of the assets (some fully realized and perhaps others only partially developed) that you bring to your future career. You've defined key characteristics about yourself, identified special interests and strengths, examined your work values, and analyzed your basic work personality traits. All in all, you've taken a good, hard look at yourself and we're hoping that you're encouraged by all the potential you've discovered.

This book offers ample opportunity for you to consider putting all that potential to work keeping the world safe. Perhaps more than ever before this heroic ideal is making its way into the career aspirations of young people in every corner of the world. In a nation where homeland security is a top priority and a world where freedom is increasingly threatened,

there is a growing demand for professionals to plan, manage, and provide a wide variety of legal and public safety services. These opportunities can be found in government at every level—local, state, and federal—as well as in corporate, industrial, and personal situations.

Overall, the job outlook for these professions is very good. According to the National Association of State Directors of Career Technical Education Consortium, "renewed national interest in public safety and security should help expand opportunities for employment in law, public

fyi Each of the following profiles includes several common elements to help guide you through an effective career exploration process. For each career, you'll find:

- A sidebar loaded with information you can use to find out more about the profession. Professional associations, pertinent reading materials, the lowdown on wages and suggested training requirements, and a list of typical types of employers are all included to give you a broader view of what the career is all about.
- An informative essay describing what the career involves.
- Get Started Now strategies you can use right now to get prepared, test the waters, and develop your skills.
- A Hire Yourself project providing realistic activities like those you would actually find on the job. Try these learning activities and find out what it's really like to be a . . . you name it.

You don't have to read the profiles in order. You may want to first browse through the career ideas that appear to be most interesting. Then check out the others—you never know what might interest you when you know more about it. As you read each profile, think about how well it matches up with what you learned about yourself in Section 1: **Discover You at Work.** Narrow down your options to a few careers and use the rating system described below to evaluate your interest levels.

- **No way!** There's not even a remote chance that this career is a good fit for me. (Since half of figuring out what you do want to do in life involves figuring out what you don't want to do, this is not a bad place to be.)
- **This is intriguing.** I want to learn more about it and look at similar careers as well. (The activities outlined in Section 3: **Experiment with Success** will be especially useful in this regard.)
- **This is it!** It's the career I've been looking for all my life and I want to go after it with all I've got. (Head straight to Section 3: **Experiment with Success.**)

safety and security. Numerous job openings will stem from employment growth attributable to increased corporate, industrial, and homeland security. Also, a more security-conscious society and concern about drug-related crimes should contribute to the increasing demand."

This book introduces a wide variety of these careers. To make it easier for you to get a handle on the wide range of opportunities, we've included careers from each of the five law and public safety career "pathways" as designated by the U.S. Department of Education. Careers in each pathway are grouped according to common types of knowledge and skills and include correction services, emergency and fire management services, legal services, law enforcement services, security and protective services. Following are descriptions of each pathway.

Correction Services

Correction services include all the careers associated with keeping society safe from criminals. Stricter enforcement of laws is expected to contribute to a whopping 36 percent increase in correctional job opportunities by the year 2010. This pathway includes professionals who work in jails, penitentiaries, and rehabilitation programs. Correction services careers profiled in this book include correctional officer and parole and probation officer.

Emergency and Fire Management Services

Emergency and fire management services is another widely recognized pathway. Whether it's a fire, a traffic accident, or a medical crisis, these are the people who come to the rescue in all kinds of emergency situations. These professions tend to attract the best and the brightest among us and these professionals generally share a common need to serve others in meaningful ways. Emergency and fire management professions profiled in this book include emergency management specialist, emergency medical technician, fire investigator, municipal firefighter, public safety diver, and wildland firefighter.

Security and Protective Services

Governments, airports, military bases, businesses, factories, and other types of public businesses depend on a variety of security and protective service professionals to keep property, people, and products safe from harm or theft. Security and protective services occupations featured in this book include fire marshal, hazardous materials technician, information systems security specialist, insurance investigator, occupational health and safety specialist, private investigator, and recreational services safety specialist.

A Note on Websites

Websites tend to move around a bit. If you have trouble finding a particular site, use an Internet browser to search for a specific website or type of information.

Law Enforcement Services

Law enforcement services keep society secure by performing tasks that range from directing traffic and patrolling neighborhoods to investigating crimes and processing crime scene evidence. Law enforcement careers profiled in this book include border patrol agent, federal special agent, forensic artist, forensic nurse, forensic pathologist, forensic science technician, humane law enforcement officer, immigration officer, police officer, public safety dispatcher, and wildlife conservation officer.

Legal Services

Our nation's legal system depends on a wide variety of legal services professionals doing their job ethically and effectively. While many of these professionals work in positions directly associated with the pursuit of justice, many others work to ensure fair and equitable processes in matters such as real estate, taxation, and estate planning. Legal service professions profiled in this book include administrative law judge, arbitrator and mediator, bailiff, court reporter, judge, lawyer, legal nurse consultant, and paralegal.

find your future
administrative law judge

administrative law judge

If every dispute and claim of legal wrong-doing had to be settled by a civil trial, our courts would be overburdened, cases would take even longer to become resolved, and the cost of bringing action against someone would be prohibitive. Fortunately, we have several systems of alternative dispute resolution (ADR). Administrative law judges (also known as hearing officers, hearing examiners, and adjudicators) represent one of these alternative systems.

There are three important distinctions common to all cases presided over by an administrative law judge (ALJ). First, all cases are civil in nature. Criminal trials are not eligible for ADR. Second, all involved parties agree to forego a jury trial in favor of allowing an administrative law judge to make decisions about the case. And, finally, all cases heard by an administrative law judge must include a government agency as one party in the dispute.

Get Started Now!

- Prepare to become a lawyer in one of the fields that relates to those addressed by administrative law judges.
- Search on-line for "administrative law judge" or "hearing officer" in your state. Learn about the requirements for the job and the types of cases they usually handle.
- ALJs have to write formal documents about the decisions they make. Take classes that require you to do formal research papers.
- Learn to communicate effectively and persuasively by participating in speech classes and debate clubs.

Search It!
The Federal Administrative Law Judges Conference at ***www.faljc.org/faljc1.html*** and National Conference of the Administrative Law Judiciary at ***www.abanet.org/jd/ncalj/home.html***

Read It!
National Association of Administrative Law Judges newsletters at ***www.naalj.org***

Learn It!
- Must be an attorney
- Must have significant experience in administrative law
- Must pass a test for federal positions

Earn It!
Median annual salary is $64,500. (Source: U.S. Department of Labor)

Find It!
Federal agencies hire administrative law judges (ALJs) from a roster maintained by the U.S. Office of Personnel Management. Check USAJOBS at ***www.usajobs.opm.gov/ei28.asp***.

Hire Yourself!

As part of the process of settling claims, administrative law judges must tell people how to appeal the decision if it goes against the individual. Go on-line to the Legal Information Institute website at ***http://supct.law.cornell.edu/supct/cases/adlaw.htm*** and review some historic administrative law cases. Select three cases and explain why you agree or disagree with the judge's decision.

According to the U.S. Office of Personnel Management, about one quarter of all ALJs work for the federal government in one of 31 different agencies. In general, their cases fall into one of three categories.

Regulatory cases usually involve agencies that regulate rates and services provided by industries vital to our economy. These agencies include the Federal Communications Commission (FCC), the Energy Regulatory Commission (ERC), and others.

Entitlement cases have to do with benefits that citizens believe they are entitled to under the law, such as disability and other compensation payable under the Social Security Act or worker's compensation payments.

Enforcement cases, the third major category, involve federal agencies attempting to enforce federal laws and regulations by bringing action against individuals or companies. Enforcement cases include those involving workplace safety (brought before the Occupational Safety and Health Review Commission), aviation safety (brought before the National Transportation Safety Board), and mine safety (brought before the Mine Safety and Health Review Commission).

In order to be eligible to apply for an administrative law judge position in the federal government, applicants must be attorneys with at least seven years administrative law experience. Qualified applicants then have to provide statements showing that they have already had positions of similar responsibility, pass tests and interviews, and provide personal references.

Administrative law judges are selected by the U.S. Office of Personnel Management and then assigned to a specific agency as the need arises. Although each judge is primarily assigned to one agency (with the Social Security Administration having by far the greatest number), individual judges may be asked to work for other agencies when there is a need.

Congress recognized that if administrative law judges were actually employed by a specific agency, it might give the government an unfair advantage—or, at the very least, raise concerns about the possibility of a judge's loyalty towards his or her employer influencing decisions. Legislators addressed this problem in two ways: by appointing federal administrative law judges to life terms and by naming the neutral Office of Personnel Management as the agency responsible for setting judges' salaries and directing performance evaluations.

Administrative law judges who work for a state have similar responsibilities to those who work for the federal government, except that their cases deal with state and local agencies. The most common types of state hearings are related to unemployment benefits, social services, child support, special education, and different types of licensing. Cases tried before these judges are usually much less formal than those tried in civil courts and many people represent themselves rather than bringing along a lawyer. The requirements to be an ALJ tend to be less strict at the state level. In some states, judges are not necessarily required to be lawyers if they have sufficient experience and expertise in a specific area. Also, state ALJs are usually appointed for a specific term and have to reapply for subsequent terms.

Search It!
American Arbitration Association at ***www.adr.org***, Federal Mediation and Conciliation Service at ***www.fmcs.gov***, and Association for Conflict Resolution at ***www.acrnet.org***

Read It!
Mediate.com at ***www.mediate.com***

Learn It!
- Associate's or bachelor's degree
- Related work experience
- Completion of approved training program for mediation

Earn It!
Median annual salary is $47,320. (Source: U.S. Department of Labor)

Find It!
About half of all arbitrators and mediators work for state and local governments. Others work for unions, law offices, insurance carriers, and companies that specialize in providing dispute resolution services.

arbitrator and mediator

Arbitration and mediation are forms of alternative dispute resolution (ADR). Chances are, you've experienced both—whether you realize it or not.

Think back to any situation where you were at odds with a friend, a sibling, or even a parent. When you were young, it might have been a dispute about whose turn it was to play with a toy. Today it might be about using the family car or who is supposed to do what chores. How was that dispute handled? Even in preschool arguments over toys, physical violence against the other person was usually not an acceptable solution. If an adult came into the situation, made a decision, and required that it be

Get Started Now!

- Does your school have a peer mediation program? If it does, sign up for it. If not, talk to your guidance counselor about starting one.
- Review ADR principles in action at websites such as the Victim Offender Mediation Association at ***www.voma.org***. And check out a program within the U.S. Postal Service to resolve discrimination conflicts at ***www.usps.com/redress***. See the Federal Mediation and Conciliation Service site at ***www.fmcs.gov*** and the Department of Justice site at ***www.usdoj.gov/crt/ada/mediate.htm*** to see examples of successful mediations.
- Join the debate team if your school has one.
- Watch political debates on television and analyze the way each candidate communicates ideas and argues important issues.

Hire Yourself!

You've been designated the official family mediator in your home. Think back (this probably won't be hard) to a situation involving conflict between two or more members of the family. Use poster board or a large sheet of paper to make a chart with four squares. In the first square, describe the general nature of the conflict. In the second square, describe the "plaintiff's" complaint and in the third square describe the "defendant's" defense. Weigh the issue carefully, and in the fourth square, describe a solution in which both parties "win."

implemented, your dispute was resolved by arbitration. If, instead, the adult led a discussion so that you and your friend or sibling could work out a compromise for yourselves, you participated in mediation.

In the adult world, some disputes are handled in similar ways. Of course, in legal matters adults might choose to hire attorneys and take the matter to court. However, this process is expensive, lengthy, and, at times, requires making matters that are best left private open to public record. In addition, since the foundation of the American legal system is an adversarial one, at least one of the disputing parties is likely to "lose" while the other one "wins." Alternative dispute resolution, on the other hand, emphasizes finding solutions to mutual problems. ADR is becoming increasingly common in landlord-tenant disputes, in labor negotiations, and even in divorce and child custody cases. Some other examples include mediation between victims and offenders, a program within the U.S. Postal Service to resolve discrimination conflicts, federal programs for family mediation, and the Department of Justice ADA Mediation Program to resolve issues related to the Americans with Disabilities Acts.

To become a professional mediator, most people begin with a 40-hour basic training and a 20-hour advanced training. A few colleges have begun to implement graduate or certificate programs in conflict resolution.

With states making ADR mandatory in certain situations and greater numbers of people voluntarily choosing arbitration or mediation, the outlook is good for future peacemakers.

Many arbitrators and mediators work as private consultants or are associated with an attorney or a law firm. Others are employees of government agencies or state or local judicial systems. All successful arbitrators and mediators are skilled negotiators, effective communicators, and well-versed in the legal issues surrounding their particular area of specialization.

Search It!
National Sheriffs' Association at ***www.sheriffs.org***

Read It!
Law and Order Magazine at ***www.lawandordermag.com***

Learn It!
- Minimum high school diploma or GED
- Many have two- or four-year degree in criminal justice or law enforcement
- Peace Officer Standards and Training Academy (POST) required in many states

Earn It!
Median annual salary is $32,700. (Source: U.S. Department of Labor)

Find It!
Most bailiffs work for state and local government court systems. Look for job leads at Careers in Government at ***www.careersingovernment.com***.

find your future bailiff

bailiff

Everyone knows that when a judge bangs the gavel on the bench, he or she expects "order in the court!" The person responsible for enforcing that order is the bailiff. A bailiff is a special type of sheriff's deputy who provides security in courtrooms. He or she informs participants of courtroom rules and makes sure people follow those rules throughout each trial. Bailiffs keep the judge, jury, and witnesses safe by looking for concealed weapons and confiscating them from people entering the court. Bailiffs also keep the courtroom calm by restraining participants who act aggressively when they don't agree with a verdict. A bailiff may have to subdue, remove, or arrest someone who does not cooperate with courtroom rules.

A big part of a bailiff's day is spent performing clerical duties and acting as the judge's assistant. Bailiffs announce the judge's entrance into the courtroom and make sure that the judge has all the appropriate files and supplies for each case. During the course of a trial, a bailiff handles articles of evidence, swears in witnesses, and escorts prisoners, juries, and witnesses to and from the courthouse. Bailiffs escort jurors to restaurants and other areas to minimize contact with the public, and when jurors are sequestered it is bailiffs who stand guard at the hotels.

Bailiffs work with people all day, every day. Good communication, interpersonal, and conflict resolution skills are really important for job

Get Started Now!

- Take courses in government, physical education, psychology, and sociology.
- Prepare for the clerical portion of the job by learning basic business computer skills, and brush up on your typing speed and accuracy.
- Watch some jury trials in your area. Pay special attention to what the bailiff does. Think about how you might react in a similar situation.

Hire Yourself!

You are the bailiff in a courtroom trial of a dog owner whose animal bit a neighbor's child. What physical evidence do you expect the attorneys to bring to the trial? How will you make sure the news media does not disturb jury members as they leave the courtroom for lunch? If the plaintiff reacts badly after he receives a guilty verdict, how will you keep him under control? Write a story about your experience.

success. Patience and physical strength can help a bailiff subdue uncooperative people if that becomes necessary. In order to keep track of a trial's progress, bailiffs should have excellent observational skills and a knowledge of and interest in the law. Since bailiffs are often called upon to work with people from a variety of cultures, they should be comfortable and nonjudgmental with people from a variety of backgrounds. And knowing another language can be a real asset.

There is no set path for becoming a bailiff. State and local court systems usually require applicants to have a high school diploma or GED, and it has become increasingly common for bailiffs to have college degrees in law enforcement or criminal justice. Many bailiffs come to the job with experience as a sheriff's deputy or police officer and learn the procedures through on-the-job training with more experienced bailiffs. Many states require all law enforcement officers, including bailiffs, to complete the Peace Officer Standards and Training Academy (POST). During this three- to six-month training period, which often takes place at a police academy, bailiff candidates learn how to use weapons, direct and control traffic, and handle emergencies. They also study the necessary skills of self-defense and first aid.

Some court systems send bailiffs to formal courtroom security schools to develop the specific skills for this job. During the month-long program, bailiffs learn procedures for working with juries, prisons, and evidence. They also learn how to protect judges and defend themselves.

Bailiffs often have to pass background checks and drug screening tests. With personality styles and judgment so critical to the job, additional screening often includes interviews or psychological tests.

Bailiffs wear uniforms similar to those of regular sheriff's deputies. There are times when the courtroom can be a dangerous place, so bailiffs often wear bulletproof vests and carry guns as part of their uniforms.

Search It!
The U.S. Bureau of Customs and Border Protection (CBP) at ***www.cbp.gov***

Read It!
Customs and border patrol news at ***www.customs.treas.gov/xp/cgov/newsroom***

Learn It!
- Bachelor's degree or adequate work experience
- Successful completion of several-week training program
- 1,500 hours' flight time for aviation enforcement officers (AEOs)

Earn It!
Median annual salary is $41,600. (Source: U.S. Department of Labor)

Find It!
Apply directly on the Customs and Border Patrol website at ***http://cbp.gov/xp/cgov/careers/careerfinder***.

border patrol agent

Unlike many countries on other continents, the continental United States shares its borders with only two other countries—Canada and Mexico. But protecting each of those two borders is no small challenge. Our border with Canada is more than 5,500 miles long, and our border with Mexico is almost 2,000 miles long! In addition to that, there are thousands of miles of maritime (ocean) borders. And that's not even accounting for air traffic coming into this country!

There is a constant activity along these invisible lines. Hundreds of millions of people cross our borders every year, and two-thirds of those people are citizens of other countries. To regulate this activity, our government employs customs and border patrol (CBP) agents.

Customs and border patrol agents have one primary responsibility: to ensure that all things and persons passing into and out of our country are doing so legally. Customs and border protection were placed under the umbrella of the Department of Homeland Security when that department was created in 2002, emphasizing how important it is to maintain our country's stability and security.

There are many different jobs for CBP agents. Pilots for the Immigration and Customs Enforcement (ICE) use complex radar and sensory equipment to locate airspace intruders, which often carry drugs into

Get Started Now!

These strategies may help you on your way to becoming a customs and border patrol agent:

- Math, science, and language classes (especially Spanish) will all come in handy.
- If you want to pursue a career as a government official, you should cultivate leadership skills. Run for class office, student government, or officer of a club.

Hire Yourself!

You have been hired by U.S. Customs and Border Protection. Your job is to become familiar with the ports of entry. Go on-line to ***www.customs.gov/xp/cgov/toolbox/ports/*** and make a detailed list of 20 ports of entry and location. Be sure to include the code and regulations affiliated with each port. This is your country, after all. Find out where all the action is!

the country. Once an illegal aircraft is detected, the pilots call for assistance and pursue the plane—often for a period of several hours. When an illegal aircraft lands, the P-3 pilot "swoops" in and arrests the offenders. Sounds pretty exciting, doesn't it? Well, an exciting job doesn't come without its costs—there are several training requirements. Candidates must receive 16 weeks of training at the Federal Law Enforcement Training Center in Glynco, Georgia. They must also be qualified to operate firearms. Military aviation surveillance experience would definitely prepare you for the job and give you an advantage over other candidates.

Other types of CBP agents patrol our land and sea borders. There are 317 official ports of entry into the United States. Port personnel are the customs workers who oversee the passage of visitors and cargo into the country, making certain that everything is legitimate. They see to it that import and export, as well as immigration laws are adhered to. Port personnel also inspect plants and livestock coming into the United States to prevent the entry of disease into the country. Agents called border patrol specialists keep illegal aliens, terrorists, weapons, drugs, and other contraband from successfully making their way into our land.

Those who specialize in imports have come to play an increasingly important role in customs and border protection. With increased global trade, the job of deciding what commodities pass inspection has become even more important. Import specialists classify and value billions of dollars' worth of commercial imports every year. They must make their decisions based on public health and safety, evaluating each situation for potential hazards. They also deal with smuggling, drug trafficking, fraud, and counterfeiting.

There are a variety of qualifications to become a customs and border patrol agent. Pilots must enlist before their 37th year (or 40th year, in the case of P-3 pilots), they must be U.S. citizens, and they must have a bachelor's degree, or three years' general work experience. Several weeks of specialized training is required of candidates of jobs in all capacities. Candidates also need to pass, with a score of 70 or above, a

written examination that tests logic and grasp of the Spanish language, as well as ability to learn the Spanish language.

That said, this is rewarding work—both in terms of compensation and day-to-day experience. Agents usually receive holiday pay, law enforcement availability pay (an additional 25% of base pay), life and health insurance, and a generous retirement package. U.S. Customs and Border Protection is actively recruiting new officers, so if you think securing your country's borders is something you'd be both good at and interested in, then now is a good time to look into it!

find your coroner future

coroner

Coroners are public officials, either elected or appointed to work in a specific city or county. The primary job of the coroner is to determine the cause of death in sudden, violent, or questionable cases. To do that, coroners direct the physicians and technologists who conduct autopsies and who analyze pathological and toxicological reports. The coroner also directs workers who prepare required legal documents.

The coroner is also involved in investigations surrounding these accidental, violent, or unexplained deaths. Often the primary goal of these investigations is to determine whether foul play or medical malpractice was involved in the death and, if so, to help determine responsibility. The investigative aspect of the coroner's job requires experience with criminal investigations, as well as strong leadership and communication skills. The investigation may require coordinating with public health and law enforcement agencies, as well as testifying at inquests, hearings, and court trials.

In situations involving suspicious deaths, the deceased person's body provides the most important clues about what happened. Autopsies involve a thorough medical examination of the tissues and organs of a deceased person to collect evidence as to the cause of death or to study any diseases that existed prior to death. The results of autopsies are

Get Started Now!

- Take classes in biology, anatomy, and chemistry.
- Take classes in public speaking to gain confidence communicating in uncomfortable situations.
- Go to the "news" section on Google.com and search for "coroner." Make a list of the various situations that coroners have been called to investigate during the past two weeks. List the different responsibilities that are part of the job in different states.

Search It!
National Association of Medical Examiners at ***www.thename.org***

Read It!
So You Want to be a Medical Detective? at ***www.thename.org/medical_detective.htm***

Learn It!
- Bachelor's degree in pre-medical subject
- Completion of pathology training and residency

Earn It!
Median annual salary is $44,140. (Source: U.S. Department of Labor) Medical examiners and coroners who are also physicians earn considerably more.

Find It!
Use the Internet to search for coroners in your state. You may find specific job openings or discover that the position is an elected one.

Hire Yourself!

Make a chart with six columns. Label the columns with the following headings: cardiovascular system, respiratory system, central nervous system, genitourinary system, liver and portal system, and gastrointestinal system. Then go on-line to the Virtual Autopsy website at ***www.le.ac.uk/pathology/teach/va/titlpag1.html***. First, click on the Anatomy and Physiology icon. Write a brief description of the functions of each of the six systems. Then preview the case studies and find a cause of death related to each of the systems and record the official cause of death in the appropriate column of your chart.

often used as evidence in murder trials in cases where medical malpractice is suspected and in court trials related to accidents involving automobiles, machinery, or other consumer products.

Once a determination of the cause of death has been made, a coroner must complete an official death certificate. Perhaps one of the toughest parts of the job involves notifying relatives of the deceased and providing information to them about the circumstances surrounding both the death and the investigative processes.

Medical examiners perform similar functions as coroners, but since they are trained physicians they are more likely to be personally involved in conducting autopsies. Their medical expertise can also provide valuable insight into the deceased's medical history and in interpreting autopsy and lab results. Medical examiners are often pathologists who specialize in forensic medicine.

correctional officer

Correctional officers are responsible for overseeing individuals in local jails and in state and federal prisons. Some individuals incarcerated in these places may have been convicted of the most violent crimes imaginable, while others may have been convicted of "white collar" crimes, such as investment fraud or embezzlement.

County and municipal jails usually house people who have recently been arrested and are awaiting trial. People actually serving time for misdemeanors (minor offenses) make up less than half of the jail population.

There is plenty of need for correctional officers in local jails. Our nation's jail system admits and processes more than 11 million people a year. Since individuals are released or transferred to prisons daily, there are only about half a million offenders in jail at any given time. Due to the transient nature of local jail populations, these jails rarely offer treatment or rehabilitative programs.

The majority of correctional officers work in large prisons. State prisons house individuals convicted of felonies, who have received sentences of one year or more. Federal prisons house those convicted of

Get Started Now!

- See what an actual prison looks like. Take the virtual prison tour from the Florida Department of Corrections at ***www.dc.state.fl.us/oth/vtour***.
- Check with your own state's prison system. See if you can get a tour or interview a correctional officer.
- Get practice enforcing rules by volunteering as an umpire or referee at children's sporting events.
- Practice keyboarding and effective writing skills.

Search It!

The Corrections Connection at ***www.corrections.com*** and American Correctional Association at ***www.aca.org***

Read It!

Corrections Today magazine at ***www.aca.org/publications/ctmagazine.asp***

Learn It!

- Minimum of high school education or equivalent
- U.S. citizen, with no felony convictions
- Bachelor's degree in criminology, psychology, or sociology helpful for advancement

Earn It!

Median annual salary is $35,090. (Source: U.S. Department of Labor)

Find It!

Jobs are posted at the American Correctional Association at ***www.aca.org/jobbank*** and at the Corrections Connection Career Center at ***http://database.corrections.com/career***.

Hire Yourself!

According to the PBS Prisons in America website (***http://www.pbs.org/now/society/prisons2.html***), there are currently more people in American prisons than ever in the nation's history. To find relevant facts and figures go on-line to the U.S. Department of Justice, Bureau of Justice Statistics at ***www.ojp.usdoj.gov/bjs/welcome.html***, the Federal Bureau of Prisons at ***www.bop.gov***, and the International Centre for Prison Studies at ***www.kcl.ac.uk/depsta/rel/icps/links-resources.html***. Use the data you discover to create a poster that accurately describes the American correctional system and its populations.

violating federal laws, such as kidnapping or bringing drugs into the country. In addition to state and federal facilities, the U.S. Immigration and Naturalization Service also holds individuals until they can be released or deported.

The primary job of correctional officers is to maintain order and to prevent escape or violence. To do that, they monitor the activities of the prisoners in all of their daily activities, including work assignments, recreational time, and meals, and they escort them to court, medical visits, or transfers to different facilities. Correctional officers keep a sharp eye on the physical facilities, looking for evidence of tampering with locks, bars, doors, and gates.

Prisons are always at risk of emergencies such as fires, fights, and riots. Correctional officers are trained to look for signs of fire hazards, unsanitary conditions, and disputes among prisoners that need to be resolved before they escalate. They also inspect mail and visitors to make sure that prohibited items do not make their way into the facility.

Most correctional officers have a high degree of personal interaction with prisoners.

However, in the highest security facilities (those with the most dangerous inmates), officers often use television cameras and a computer tracking system to monitor prisoners from a central remote control center.

Correctional officers are constantly reporting on conditions in their area. They keep a daily log of their activities and report the conduct and activity of individual inmates as well as on all unusual occurrences.

What does it take to be a correctional officer? Commitment to doing an excellent job is an especially welcome trait. It also takes excellent communication skills. Correctional officers who work directly with prisoners may be unarmed. Thus, their interpersonal skills are often their primary tool for enforcing regulations. Flexibility is another important job trait.

Applicants for correctional officer positions must show a history of job stability. They must be in good health, and meet formal standards of physical fitness, eyesight, and hearing. They have to show that they can be calm in a crisis, make fast and responsible decisions, and think and react quickly. They must also pass a written examination, drug tests, and background checks.

New correctional officers often train at regional training academies followed by several weeks or months of on-the-job training at the local facility. Training generally includes institutional policies, regulations, operations, and custody and security procedures, as well as legal restrictions, interpersonal relations, firearms proficiency, and self-defense skills. Federal correctional officers must complete 120 hours of specialized training at the U.S. Federal Bureau of Prisons residential training center in Georgia within the first 60 days after appointment and then undergo an additional 200 hours of formal training within the first year of employment.

Search It!
National Court Reporters Association at ***www.ncraonline.org*** and National Verbatim Reporters Association at ***www.nvra.org***

Read It!
A Resource for the Online Court Reporter at ***www.depoman.com*** and the history of court reporting at ***www.bestfuture.com/history.htm***

Learn It!
- One- to two-year specialized training in vocational or technical school
- Exceptional keyboard skills

Earn It!
Median annual salary is $41,600 per year.
(Source: U.S. Department of Labor)

Find It!
Find job listings posted at the National Court Reporters Association at ***www.ncraonline.org/classifiedads***.

court reporter

Court reporters have front row seats in court rooms across America. It's their job to record and document every word spoken in a trial and other types of legal proceedings.

Since court reporters use machines, including sophisticated voice recognition computers, it's easy to think that this is a relatively new profession.

But long before the American legal system ever existed, Roman orators and leaders, such as Cicero, wanted to have their speeches recorded precisely. Marcus Tullius, a freed slave, used a system of shorthand to record these speeches as far back as the fourth century B.C. We still use some of the shorthand symbols Tullius devised, like the ampersand (the familiar "&" symbol).

Today there are two main methods of court reporting: stenotyping and voice writing.

Stenotyping is the method commonly seen in television courtroom scenes, where the court reporter types into a small machine. This stenotyping machine allows the operator to press multiple keys at a time so that he or she can record combinations of letters representing different

Get Started Now!

- Learn about the history of computer-aided transcription (CAT) at ***www.ncraonline.org/about/history/CAT.shtml***.
- One of the most most important skills for court reporters is a command of the English language. Be sure to hone your good grammar, vocabulary, and punctuation in English and composition courses.
- Court reporters need accurate and fast keyboarding classes. Brush up on your own skills by taking computer skills or practice on-line with free typing lessons at ***www.senselang.com/Typing/keynet.html***.

Hire Yourself!

As a court reporter, you should be very familiar with the words that come up most often. Look at relevant websites to learn legal terminology. The Legal Dictionary at ***www.nolo.com*** is a good place to start. Use this and other resources you find on-line to create a personal law dictionary in a notebook or use your favorite computer word processing software.

sounds, words, or phrases. Sometimes we see the court reporter hold up part of the printout that the machine produces in order to read back part of the trial to the courtroom. What we don't see is what happened at the end of the day, when the stenotypist would take this very long printout and use a typewriter to transcribe the symbols into readable English.

Today, that typing step has largely been eliminated. The symbols that are typed into the stenograph machine are recorded directly onto CD-ROM disks, which are put into a computer that uses a process called computer-aided transcription to turn them into regular text.

In some situations, even computer-aided transcription is not fast enough. That's where CART (communications access real-time translation) comes in. CART allows stenotype machines to be directly connected to the computer. As a reporter keys in the symbols they instantly appear as text on a computer screen or even on a large projection screen. Although CART makes trials faster, more efficient, and less expensive, the technology is also used for reasons other than speed. It permits lawyers to send testimony by modem and get advice from colleagues, assistants, or experts in their office or even in another state. In areas where computer-integrated courtrooms have been created, it is now possible for hearing-impaired people to read the screen instantaneously, enabling them to participate fully in legal matters as witnesses, jurors, lawyers and even as judges. Real-time has also been used throughout the United States to caption political speeches and presidential addresses, congressional hearings, conventions and meetings, and college classes.

Voice writing, the second method of court reporting, uses a piece of equipment called a stenomask—a mouth mask with a built-in microphone. The stenomask allows the court reporter to speak without being heard by other people, and keeps background noise away from the microphone. Reporters using voice writing techniques not only have to repeat everything said by each person in the courtroom (including judges, witnesses, and attorneys), but they also have to indicate who is speaking, and describe gestures that are made and emotional reactions.

It takes a lot of focus to pay attention to everything, repeat every word you hear as you hear it, and memorize the next things that are being said all at the same time.

Of course, good court reporters are very fast in their note taking (or voice writing) and transcribing. But speed alone does not make for a successful court reporter. The most important quality is accuracy. Remember, there is only one "official" transcript of each proceeding—the one that the court reporter supplies. In a courtroom situation, appeals and jury decisions often depend on the court reporter's transcript. Accurate transcription of depositions (sworn testimony that is given before a trial begins or when a witness is unable to attend the actual court session) is equally important.

The future for court reporters is positive. While technology is now used to automate many parts of the process, there will always be a need for people who can operate the technology and manage the processes. Federal regulations have also increased the need for stenocaptioners, the reporters who record live television shows for captioning.

Requirements for becoming a court reporter vary by state. Some states require Certified Court Reporter (CCR) certification, some require court reporters to be notary publics, and some require testing and state licensing.

find your future

emergency management specialist

emergency management specialist

When disasters such as floods, earthquakes, or terrorist attacks occur, time is of the essence. Knowing what to do when the worst happens saves lives and minimizes damage. Rather than being caught off-guard when a crisis strikes, emergency management specialists craft detailed warning, control, and evacuation plans. They train others to use these plans, and during an emergency, they may act as leaders or members of disaster response teams.

In the past, most disasters were natural, like floods, hurricanes, and tornadoes, or were accidental like fires and power outages. However, since the terrorist attacks on September 11, 2001, the scope of an emergency management specialist's job has widened considerably. Most emergency management specialists work as employees or contractors for federal or local governments. Others work independently as consultants to help businesses, utility companies, and other organizations prepare for emergencies.

Get Started Now!

- Take math classes like algebra, geometry, and trigonometry to develop logic and analytical skills.
- Familiarize yourself with the emergency management agency in your own city or state. Search for your local agency at ***www.emergencymanagement.org/state-em.html***.
- Practice managing large groups of people by getting involved in student government or becoming a leader in school clubs.

Search It!

National Emergency Management Association at ***www.nemaweb.org***, National Safety Council at ***www.nsc.org/issues/prepare.htm***, and Federal Emergency Management Agency at ***www.fema.gov***

Read It!

Contingency Planning & Management magazine at ***www.contingencyplanning.com***

Learn It!

- Bachelor's or master's degree required
- Prior work or military experience

Earn It!

Median annual salary is $43,560. (Source: U.S. Department of Labor)

Find It!

Emergency management specialists work for federal, state, and local government agencies, nonprofit organizations, and businesses. Find federal jobs at the Federal Emergency Management Agency site at ***www.fema.gov/career/index.jsp***.

Hire Yourself!

You have been hired as the emergency management specialist for your school district. Develop a presentation that clearly explains how your school should respond in the case of a hurricane, earthquake, or flash flood. Your presentation should include:

- Plans for training and practice exercises
- Safety measures or equipment you will have in place ahead of time
- Destination, including the best and safest route to it, if evacuation is necessary
- Plans for communication within the school before and during the emergency
- Educating parents about what they should do and where students will be taken

To begin planning for a crisis situation, emergency management specialists start by conducting surveys or assessments of their clients to determine specific emergency-related needs. The scope of a crisis management plan may be as narrow as an individual school, hospital, manufacturing plant, or business, or as broad as an entire city or mass transit system. Each situation involves similarities and differences—the needs of each depending on the type of organization and its location. For example, a school in California might be concerned about safely evacuating hundreds of children in the event of an earthquake, while a government building in Washington, D.C., may prioritize the importance of protecting employees in the event of an enemy attack.

After emergency management specialists develop a plan, they test it by holding "tabletop exercises," a type of virtual reality drill where every possible scenario is thoroughly examined to ensure that the plan is as comprehensive as possible. Eventually, they hold mock disaster situations that simulate possible emergencies as closely as possible and provide practice runs for disaster response teams.

Emergency management specialists inspect a client's facilities and equipment to search for pitfalls that might make the plan less effective, and they keep up with federal, state, and local regulations that might affect emergency plans. For instance, one of many vital lessons learned in the aftermath of 9/11 concerned people with physical conditions that made it difficult or even impossible to use stairs. With elevators unavailable, these people had to rely on the kindness of their heroic coworkers to transport them down many flights of stairs. Now, all fire exits in all federal buildings are equipped with sled-like devices that make it easy to safely and quickly transport people with disabilities in the event of emergencies.

Once an emergency plan is tested and refined, emergency management specialists hold training sessions to teach clients how to respond in the event of a disaster. After all, a crisis management plan is only words on paper unless the people potentially impacted by the crisis know what to do, where to go, and who to call when disaster strikes. These training sessions might also involve teaching clients how to use special equipment such as nuclear, biological, and chemical detection and decontamination devices.

Good communication skills are important for helping emergency management specialists express their ideas clearly and concisely to clients. The work is extremely detail-oriented and at times can be the source of a great deal of stress. The best candidates for this type of work are methodical, level-headed, and focused. The ability to stay cool, calm, and collected during the worst of situations is mandatory.

Many emergency management specialists get started on their career path through previous work experience, such as a job in security or doing similar work in the military. Although many employers required only a high school diploma in the past, many now require applicants to have extensive work experience along with a bachelor's degree in emergency planning. A small number of four-year colleges and universities now offer degrees in this area. With the current strong demand for people with this type of expertise, the number of colleges offering programs in emergency management and planning is growing.

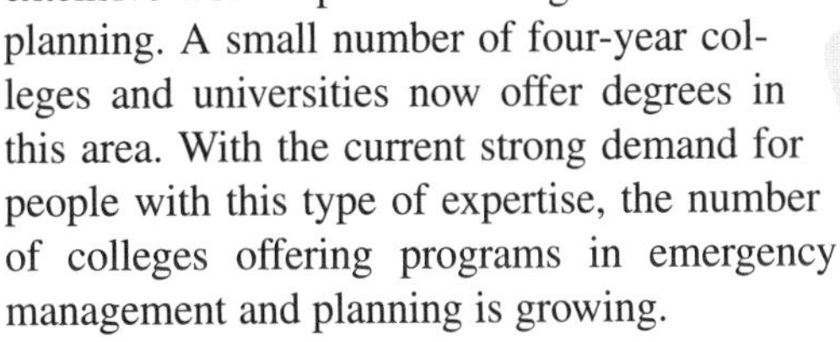

find your future
emergency medical technician

Search It!
National Association of Emergency Medical Technicians at ***www.naemt.org***

Read It!
Emergency Medical Services magazine at ***www.emsmagazine.com***

Learn It!
- EMT certification programs available at community colleges, hospitals, and health care trade schools
- On-the-job training

Earn It!
Median annual salary is $24,030. (Source: U.S. Department of Labor)

Find It!
EMTs usually work for private ambulance companies or local public service organizations such as fire, police, or rescue squads. Look for job leads at ***http://911HotJobs.com.***

emergency medical technician

At the scene of a serious accident or sudden illness, an emergency medical technician (EMT) can literally be a lifesaver. These technicians are trained to administer immediate medical attention to victims of heart attacks, drownings, gunshot wounds, and countless other emergencies. They are often the first people to respond to a medical crisis and must make speedy observations and confident decisions while rushing sick or injured patients to a hospital. It can be a highly stressful job, but many EMTs thrive on the excitement and rewarding prospects of helping to save lives.

An EMT's adventure starts as soon as he or she receives a dispatch call from a 911 operator. After learning the nature of an emergency, the EMT may ride to the scene in an ambulance with fellow technicians, in a police car, or in a fire engine with other emergency personnel. At the scene, the EMT assesses each patient's condition and administers medical care or life support following a strict set of guidelines. He or she

Get Started Now!

To get your EMT career on the fast track, start now by doing the following:

- Take courses in biology, chemistry, mathematics, first aid, and foreign language.
- Volunteer at your local rescue squad or hospital.
- Sign up for CPR and first aid classes offered through your local Red Cross chapter.
- See if your state has a Web page for their EMS department. Search for "EMS" plus the name of your state.

Hire Yourself!

You are an EMT and have been invited to speak about injury prevention by the football coach at a local middle school. He wants you to introduce five common sports injuries. Use information you find at Health World Online at ***www.healthy.net/clinic/firstaid/*** and other resources to compile your list. Then, using a separate index card for each injury, record injury prevention tips on one side and injury response tips on the other.

may have to use special equipment to treat a patient, such as external defibrillators, EKGs, and bag-valve mask resuscitators. EMTs need to know how to minimize further injury if circumstances make it necessary to transport a victim to the hospital. Usually one EMT drives the ambulance, while another continues to treat, comfort, and reassure the patient. The ambulance ride may include emergency procedures such as stomach suction, airway management, and administration of drugs or intravenous medications (under a physician's direction). EMTs have even delivered babies for mothers who could not wait until they arrived at the hospital.

At the hospital, EMTs brief doctors on the victim's condition and transfer the patient's care to emergency room staff. Then they take time to write and file written reports and clean and restock equipment. In situations where they transported a patient with a contagious illness, EMTs have to decontaminate the inside of their ambulance and report cases to the proper authorities.

To become an EMT, applicants have to undergo formal training through a certification program. Most programs offer four levels of training, from "basic" through "paramedic" level. Firefighters and police officers are often classified as EMT First Responders and have about 40 hours of training. An EMT-Basic (or EMT-1) has about 110 hours of training and can take on more responsibility. EMT-Intermediates, with about 200 to 400 hours of training, are permitted to use more of the emergency equipment. Paramedics, the highest level of EMTs, have completed 1,000 or more hours of training, can do many more procedures, and can administer drugs and IVs. Although all states require EMTs to become certified, the requirements for certification differ from state to state. Some states administer their own certification examination, and others use a standard exam given by the National Registry of Emergency Medical Technicians. In most states, EMT certification must be renewed every two years.

EMTs who thrive in their work have especially good observation and communication skills. A basic understanding of science and math are important to understanding medical issues, and speaking a foreign language can help EMTs treat people from other cultures. Physical strength is also required to handle the demands of the job. In addition, EMTs need ample supplies of emotional stamina to deal with the job stress of being exposed to life-or-death situations.

Besides the opportunity to help others, EMTs enjoy especially strong job security. The need for EMTs will continue to grow with the population, particularly in urban areas.

federal special agent

There are so many television shows about the FBI (Federal Bureau of Investigation) that it's sometimes confusing as to what the FBI actually does.

On March 1, 2003, the FBI was one of 22 different government organizations that became part of the newly organized Department of Homeland Security (although the FBI has been around since 1908). As part of this new department, one of the FBI's top priorities is to protect the United States from terrorist attacks. Other aspects of the FBI's role in national security are to protect the United States against foreign intelligence operations and espionage and to protect us from cyber-based attacks and high-tech crimes.

In addition to protecting our country from outside forces, the FBI plays a critical role in combating public corruption at all levels, civil rights violations, transnational and national criminal organizations and enterprises, major white-collar crime, and significant violent crime. The FBI also provides essential law enforcement support to a variety of federal, state, county, municipal, and even international partners.

Becoming an FBI agent requires a rigorous application and screening process, which includes fitness, vision, color vision, and hearing tests. Then there's the interview, the background check, and the polygraph test.

Get Started Now!

- For one agent's personal story, go to ***www.fbi.gov/kids/6th12th/daynlife/daynlife.htm***.
- Take classes in speech and communication. Special Agents often have to testify in court as expert witnesses.
- Work on your writing skills. You will have to submit reports that are clear, concise, and grammatically correct.

Search It!
Federal Bureau of Investigation home page at ***www.fbi.gov***

Read It!
Read about the history of the FBI at ***www.fbi.gov/libref/historic/history/historymain.htm***

Learn It!
- Four-year college degree
- At least three years of professional work experience
- Pass a physical fitness test and meet hearing and vision requirements
- U.S. citizen, between the ages of 23 and 36, and available for assignment anywhere in the FBI's jurisdiction

Earn It!
The average starting salary is $49,000.
(Source: U.S. Department of Labor)

Find It!
FBI jobs are listed at ***www.fbijobs.com***.

Hire Yourself!

You are a special agent for the FBI. You have been selected to visit local colleges and encourage students to think about careers in the FBI. Make a list of the things that might appeal to a college student about this career. Make a chart showing the differences between the FBI (***www.fbi.gov***), the Central Intelligence Agency (***www.cia.gov***), and the Secret Service (***www.ustreas.gov/usss***).

The FBI will verify an applicant's educational achievements, do credit and arrest checks, and talk to personal and business references, past employers, neighbors, and other associates. If an applicant has been convicted of a felony or major misdemeanor, uses illegal drugs, or failed to pass a drug-screening test, he or she cannot be considered for a position in the FBI.

Once accepted into the program, new recruits join a class of special agent trainees at the FBI Academy in Quantico, Virginia for a 16-week training program. The 708-hour course includes intensive training in physical fitness, defensive tactics, practical application exercises, and the use of firearms in addition to classroom programs in academics and investigative techniques. Upon graduating from the academy, new agents begin a two-year probationary period that includes periodic in-service seminars.

The actual job of special agents is extremely varied. Many days they may work outside of the office, interviewing people or looking for evi-

dence for ongoing investigations. Other times, they work inside, completing reports and doing research for other investigations. They may also review crime scene photos and case materials to prepare an analysis for another requesting agency or meet with investigators or prosecutors to discuss cases. On any given day, emergency calls from other FBI offices, local police, prosecutors, etc., determine a special agent's plans.

A specific FBI job that is often portrayed on television is that of profiler. Profilers actually work for a federal law enforcement division called the National Center for the Analysis of Violent Crime (NCAVC) and must have a minimum of three years experience as a FBI agent. Profiling is part of an exciting world of investigation and research—a world of inductive and deductive reasoning, crime-solving experience, and extensive knowledge of criminal behavior.

In addition to constructing "profiles" (descriptions of the traits and characteristics of unknown offenders in specific cases), the NCAVC staff provides many services to law enforcement agencies around the world. These services include major case management advice, threat assessment, and strategies for investigation, interviewing, or prosecution.

NCAVC special agents also share results of research and general information about the unit and services through presentations to such audiences as professional conferences or law enforcement training programs. In addition, staff members publish articles in professional journals regarding research and practices of the NCAVC.

Search It
International Association of Arson Investigators, Inc. (IAAI) at ***www.firearson.com***

Read It!
Fire Findings at ***www.firefindings.com*** and Fire and Arson Investigation resources at ***www.interfire.org/resourcecenter.asp***

Learn It!
- High school diploma or GED
- Experience as a firefighter or associate's or bachelor's degree in fire science

Earn It!
Median annual salary is $45,010 per year.
(Source: U.S. Department of Labor)

Find It!
Fire investigators work for municipalities, fire or police departments, and state and federal agencies. They also work for insurance companies, attorneys, and private investigators.

fire investigator

According to statistics from the National Fire Protection Association, about 2 million fires break out each year in the United States, killing around 4,000 people. About 25 percent of these fires are related to arson, the criminal offense of intentionally starting a fire. Most of the rest are the result of carelessness in taking care of property, which can also be considered criminal negligence. Others are caused by natural phenomena, such as lightning strikes.

Fire investigators are responsible for determining the cause of the fire. They are experienced and highly trained in the science of fires. They use this expertise and experience to determine whether the fire was caused intentionally. If it was, they work with other authorities to find and apprehend the person who caused it.

Fire investigators are puzzle solvers and often work on explosions as well as fires. They have to know about accelerants (the materials used to start or promote the spread of a fire), building construction and materials, chemical reactions of different materials, fire behavior, and burn patterns. They examine the entire fire site, collecting evidence such as glass, metal fragments, charred wood, and accelerant residue, and they save the evidence in ways that ensure its preservation. They also have to photograph the fire scene, all damage, and all evidence. They dust

Get Started Now!

- Prevention of arson is extremely important. See what your state is doing to prevent arson and identify arsonists. Try the state links at ***www.firemarshals.org/links/sfmsites.html***.
- Talk the talk! Become familiar with the terms used by fire and arson investigators at ***www.interfire.org/res_file/aec_glos.asp***.
- Contact your local fire department and ask to interview a fire investigator.

Hire Yourself!

Fire investigators have to know pretty much everything there is to know about fire. Use information you find about fire at the How Stuff Works website (***http://science.howstuffworks.com/fire.htm***) and other on-line resources to create a five- to 10-slide PowerPoint presentation about how even a simple spark of fire can cause enormous damage.

dence and the crime scene for latent fingerprints, run tests on pieces of evidence, and interview witnesses.

While fire investigators work the scene, many other specialists are also on site (or playing background roles). Depending on the size and location of the fire, there may be companies supplying everything from emergency fencing, lighting, and power sources, to food, water, and sanitation for the investigation workers. Other companies may help to board up buildings, remove hazardous materials and debris, and ensure the safety of utility hookups. To assist with the investigation itself, canine handlers may participate with dogs trained to sniff out accelerants, and forensic chemists and crime scene technicians may help collect and test evidence. Community organizations and interpreters join the investigation to help with interviews.

It's especially important that every detail of a fire investigation is handled with absolute legal integrity so that all aspects of the investigation hold up in court proceedings. An estimated 500,000 fires resulting in more than $2 billion in damage are caused by arson each year. Bringing a suspected arsonist to justice often depends on the testimony fire investigators provide in court. They must know all of the rules for obtaining evidence legally, how to document findings correctly, and how to most effectively present their evidence at a trial.

Most fire investigators find it useful to become active in as many professional organizations as possible. They go to conferences and continue to update their training through courses available from the Bureau of Alcohol, Tobacco, Firearms and Explosives; the FBI; the National Fire Academy; and programs in their own state or city.

find your future fire marshal

Search It!
National Fire Protection Association at ***www.nfpa.org*** and National Association of State Fire Marshals at ***www.firemarshals.org***

Read It!
Download all kinds of resources at the International Association of Fire Chiefs website at ***www.iafc.org/publications/documents.asp***.

Learn It!
- High school diploma or GED
- Experience as a firefighter or an associate's or bachelor's degree in fire science

Earn It!
Median annual salary is $55,450. (Source: U.S. Department of Labor)

Find It!
Look for jobs through your local or state fire prevention department or on websites such as America's JobBank at ***www.jobsearch.org***.

fire marshal

Almost every fire department has a fire prevention division, headed by a fire marshal and staffed by fire inspectors. Fire marshals help set or adapt the fire codes in an area. They are responsible for determining the number of people that can safely be in a restaurant or theater, for developing guidelines for fire drills, and for setting guidelines for programs such as false alarm billing and inspection schedules. In addition, fire marshals supervise the work of fire inspectors, who ensure that all of the fire codes are followed.

Most states have a state fire marshal. Although specific duties may differ, their general responsibilities include public education, keeping the state's safety code up to date, ensuring that all local fire departments have adequate local codes and enforcement, and advising the governor and state legislature on issues regarding fire protection. In some states, the state fire marshal's department is also responsible for investigating fires and arson, training firefighters, controlling wildland fires, and regulating natural gas and other pipelines. The top fire prevention officer for each state is usually appointed by the governor or by another high-ranking state official.

Fire marshals and fire inspectors are educators as well. They present and explain fire code requirements and fire prevention information to

Get Started Now!

- Search the Internet. Look for colleges, universities, and other schools that offer courses in fire engineering, fire control, or fire science.
- Contact your local fire department to arrange a facility tour, interview, or volunteer experience.
- Fire inspectors often have to testify in court about violations they have found. Take public speaking classes that will require you to report directly, clearly, and professionally.

Hire Yourself!

Who was Mrs. O'Leary and what did her cow have to do with the Great Chicago fire? Use websites like ***www.chicagohs.org/fire/oleary*** to find out about this and other famous fires. Make sure to investigate the San Francisco earthquake of 1906.

architects, contractors, attorneys, engineers, developers, and fire service personnel, as well as to the general public. They develop and present fire prevention programs in schools and other public places.

Fire marshals usually have several years of firefighting experience behind them before they apply for this job. Although they have become familiar with many building codes and other fire regulations during their firefighting careers, new inspectors are still trained in the details of the codes, in inspection techniques, and in implementation procedures. This training can be on-the-job (supervised by an experienced inspector or supervisor), at a college fire-training program, or through the National Fire Academy (***www.usfa.fema.gov/fire-service***).

Fire prevention begins even before a new building is erected. During preliminary planning sessions, fire inspectors review blueprints and plans to ensure that the intended structure will meet all fire codes. They look for the use of approved wiring and building materials, fire detection systems, sprinklers, fire exit routes, storage facilities for flammable materials, and other safety measures. As construction proceeds, the fire inspectors keep inspecting. No construction can continue without their approval, and no building can be occupied without their certification.

After public buildings are constructed, fire marshals continue to monitor adherence to fire prevention regulations. Marshals constantly check schools, office buildings, manufacturing plants, theaters, stores, restaurants, storage facilities, hospitals, prisons, recreational facilities, and gas stations to make sure that they are up to code. They test required systems to make sure they are working, and check to see if fire escape routes are posted and exits are accessible. They also look for hazardous conditions, such as an accumulation of combustible materials or electrical wiring problems.

Prospective fire marshals can expect to face keen competition for these coveted positions. As is the case with other types of firefighting jobs, fire marshals enjoy the challenge and opportunity to devote themselves to work that so greatly benefits their communities.

Search It!
The International Association for Identification at ***www.theiai.org***

Read It!
Neville's Forensic Art Service at ***www.forensicartist.com*** and *Forensic Artist* at ***www.ocsoartist.com/forensic_artist_Article.htm***

Learn It!
- Certification from the International Association of Identification (***www.theiai.org/certifications/artist/index.html***) is recommended
- Experience as a police officer helpful but not necessarily required

Earn It!
Median annual salary is $42,270. (Source: U.S. Department of Labor)

Find It!
Check with your local police organization. Or, see if there is a local chapter of the International Association of Identification at ***www.theiai.org/divisions/links.html***.

find your future: forensic artist

forensic artist

Forensic artists, sometimes called police artists or sketch artists, have helped capture criminals for a very long time. Before modern photography and "mug shots," artists made the sketches for the "Wanted Dead or Alive" posters that were seen throughout the Old West.

Today's forensic artists create similar sketches based on the input of victims or witnesses. These sketches are known as composite drawings. The success of the picture the forensic artist creates will depend on both the artist's technical drawing skill and his or her ability to illicit accurate descriptions from witnesses. The artist counts on the memory of eyewitness descriptions to create each aspect of a suspect's face. Once all the features are sketched the artist creates a complete picture, or "composite," of the suspect's face. Forensic artists are often called upon to do age progressions. By using their knowledge of how faces generally change as people age, combined with family information when available, forensic artists can give a good approximation of how someone would look at a later age. This is especially valuable when looking for missing children, or when looking for suspects after many years have passed. They may do other image modifications as well, adding or subtracting beards, moustaches, or eyeglasses, or changing hair color and

Get Started Now!

- Get a sketchbook and practice sketching the faces of people you know.
- Go through family albums. Observe how features change as a person ages.
- Search for websites on crime scene photography such as the "special topics" section of SCETV's Crime to Court home page at ***www.scetv.org/crimetocourt*** or at Crime Scene Investigation at ***www.crime-scene-investigator.net***.

Hire Yourself!

See how good a witness you would make! Try BlackDog's IdentiKit Game at ***www.blackdog.net/refrigerator/identi-kit***. Although this game uses outrageous cartoon features, you may be amazed at how hard it is for you to reproduce the face you've seen. After you've finished playing the on-line game, try to sketch or describe the face. Print out a copy of the on-line version and compare the results.

styles. That ability really helps law enforcement officers and the general public recognize people who may be trying to avoid recognition.

Sometimes police find remains of people that they cannot identify. There may be significant decomposition or bruising, or there may be nothing more than a skull to work with. Here, again, forensic artists and sculptors come to the rescue, creating two- or three-dimensional reconstructions.

In the 1950s, law enforcement officers thought it might be easier to standardize the creation of composite pictures, and a tool called Identi-KIT was used by many agencies. Identi-KIT was a collection of clear sheets featuring sketches of different versions of one facial feature on each sheet. The idea was that witnesses would identify the right eyes, nose, mouth, and so on, so that when all of the features were laid on top of each other, the result looked like the missing suspect or witness. Today, similar techniques are available in software programs. Rather than ask the witness to identify individual parts of the face, these software programs present a completed face based on the witness' description, and then the artist and witness make adjustments together. Using these types of programs artists can instantly change features so that, as witnesses recall more details, they can perfect the results. This type of software also allows artists to easily shift to profile or three-quarter view, make changes in styles of hair, and add more subtle identifiers.

No matter how good a natural artist a person may be, specialized training is critical to becoming a forensic artist. Forensic artists need to learn about patterns common to faces in the aging process, how the anatomy of a skull relates to the appearance of a face, and so on.

Many forensic artists become law enforcement officers first. Others take civilian jobs with the police force to have the experience of learning what criminal investigations are like and to develop a personal relationship with the detectives. While there are no specific educational requirements for this career, most agencies prefer hiring people certified by the International Association for Identification.

find your future

forensic nurse

Search It!
International Association of Forensic Nurses at ***www.forensicnurse.org***

Read It!
Forensic Nurse magazine at ***www.forensicnursemag.com***

Learn It!
- Must be an experienced registered nurse
- Minimum of a four-year bachelor's degree in nursing
- Specialized forensic training in college classes or graduate programs

Earn It!
Median annual salary is $49,550. (Source: U.S. Department of Labor)

Find It!
Forensic nurses work in hospitals and emergency care clinics, correctional facilities, and other settings. Find job leads at sites like ***http://jobsearch.nursingworld.monster.com***.

forensic nurse During the course of providing care for patients, many nurses encounter evidence of abuse, neglect, sexual assault, and other crimes. And, of course, emergency room nurses and doctors often provide care for both victims and perpetrators of crimes. In the past, much of this evidence, which can be extremely valuable to law enforcement agents, was not documented or was inadvertently destroyed. While it is a priority for crime victims or perpetrators to receive appropriate care and immediate treatment, forensic nurses are now trained to identify, collect, and properly preserve all evidence at the same time as they care for people.

The first step in gathering evidence is interviewing the patient. In addition to the usual questions about health and medical history (such as whether a patient has allergies, is taking any medications, or has a history of health problems), the forensic nurse also gets a detailed account of the crime. Knowing more about the crime gives the nurse more clues about where to focus during the next two steps: conducting a physical examination and collecting evidence. During the exam, the nurse uses cameras, evidence collection kits, and other equipment. Evidence may include samples of body fluids, fibers, blood, mud, and other clues found on the patient. Special lights and dyes allow forensic nurses to get a better view of bruises or cuts and detect miniscule quantities of blood and other fluids. After evidence collection and treatment

Get Started Now!

- Take courses in biology, chemistry, and health sciences to prepare for a career in nursing.
- Enroll in psychology and sociology classes to gain insight into human nature.
- Read news articles about important court cases to learn about the types of evidence that helps police solve cases.

Hire Yourself!

As a forensic nurse, you have been called to investigate an elderly patient in a nursing home who may be a victim of abuse. The patient is partially paralyzed from a previous stroke and cannot communicate. What evidence of elder abuse might you look for? How would you document any signs of abuse? Prepare a presentation with descriptions and sketches of evidence you found to give to law enforcement officials.

are complete, the patient is either admitted to the hospital for further treatment or discharged.

If the patient is discharged, the forensic nurse may counsel the patient about mental health issues, social services, or continuing medical care. Sometimes the nurse gives the patient a packet containing appropriate pamphlets and other information. If necessary, the forensic nurse arranges for follow-up appointments with a doctor, social worker, or other health professional.

After the examination, all evidence collected from the patient is turned over to law enforcement agents, along with reports about the patient's statements and where the evidence was found, etc. If the crime goes to trial, the forensic nurse could be called upon to act as an expert witness, testifying about observations or activities.

Discussing a violent crime can be extremely difficult and stressful for both the nurse and the victim. Patience, good communication skills, and sensitivity to others' needs are important qualities in forensic nursing. Knowing a foreign language can give nurses an edge when treating patients who are not native English speakers. Good observational skills and a familiarity with the law can help forensic nurses get the right information to law enforcement officers.

All forensic nurses are registered nurses with a minimum of a bachelor's degree. Additional training needed for a forensic specialty depends on the setting in which the nurse intends to practice. Many forensic nurses train on the job.

Forensic nurses can work in a wide variety of places including hospitals, emergency care clinics, and doctors' offices. Others specialize in correctional facilities, where they care for perpetrators of crimes, or schools, where they evaluate and treat physically and sexually abused children. A few forensic nurses work in coroner's offices, where they help evaluate time and cause of death and identify preexisting medical conditions.

forensic pathologist

Pathologists are specialized physicians who study disease. They focus on the causes, development, and progress of disease, and how the body is affected. While many pathologists study the organs and tissues of living patients to help make diagnoses and establish treatment plans, forensic (or autopsy) pathologists do similar work for the purpose of determining the cause of death. Their work includes anatomic pathology (study of the body and cells themselves) and clinical pathology (study of blood, immunology, hematology, and toxicology).

Forensic pathologists perform autopsies when requested by the coroner or medical examiner. About half the deaths examined by forensic pathologists are not the result of violent deaths such as homicides or suicides. Forensic pathologists are called in for other categories of deaths, including any deaths caused by accidents, those that are suspicious, sudden, or unexpected. The deaths of children and infants and deaths of prisoners or others under the care of an institution often require the attention of a forensic pathologist. They also investigate deaths in which illicit drugs or alcohol may have contributed, deaths during a surgical procedure, and deaths in which there is concern of a public health threat.

Forensic pathologists have to be well versed in many sciences other than traditional medicine. As they investigate crime scenes or perform autopsies, they collect body secretions and trace evidence, such as hairs, fibers, and fabrics. Because forensic pathologists order the procedures

Get Started Now!

- Take courses in biology, psychology, chemistry, and government to prepare for college and medical school.
- Watch forensic science shows on TV to get a general idea of what working in the field is like (minus all the glamour and romance, of course).
- Search a bookstore or library for books on forensics.

Search It!
National Association of Medical Examiners (NAME) at ***www.thename.org***

Read It!
Young Forensic Scientist Forum newsletter at ***www.aafs.org/yfsf/index.htm*** and the FBI's *Handbook of Forensic Services* at ***www.fbi.gov/hq/lab/handbook/intro.htm***

Learn It!
- Bachelor's degree, plus four years of medical school
- Three- to five-year residency training program in general pathology
- One year specialized training at a medical examiner's or coroner's office

Earn It!
Median annual salary is $184,000. (Source: American Medical Association)

Find It!
Look for jobs at ***www.thename.org/jobs_index.htm*** and ***www.sciencejobs.com***.

Hire Yourself!

What exactly is an autopsy? Go on-line to the American Medical Association's website and find their very informative on-line booklet called "Autopsy: Life's Final Chapter" at ***www.ama-assn.org/ama/pub/category/7635.html#1***. Use the information you find there and through other resources to create a flowchart that illustrates what the process involves from beginning to end.

that are done in the labs, they need to be very familiar with DNA technology, toxicology testing, firearms analysis (including wound ballistics), and other tests.

In addition to determining the cause of death, forensic pathologists are often called upon to determine the identity of the dead person. He or she serves a critical purpose in situations known as mass disasters (plane crashes, building collapses), where there are many bodies in one place, sorting out the body parts and trying to identify all of the victims.

Forensic pathologists not only solve the mystery behind many deaths, they also help to prevent future deaths. Their investigations can lead to changes in public health information, such as finding causes for SIDS (Sudden Infant Death Syndrome), or identifying clothing or equipment that can lead to the death of young children. Investigations of deaths from auto accidents can lead to design changes that increase rates of survival. Investigations of other unexpected deaths can reveal epidemics, poisonings, or other potential risks.

A forensic pathologist essentially fulfills two important roles associated with the medical and justice systems—that of physician and that of detective. Although there will never be a huge demand for forensic pathologists, the field is expected to grow faster than average over the next several years due to a growing population and increasing use of forensic testimony in court cases.

find your future
forensic science technician

forensic science technician

Forensic science is a hot topic for the television industry. From the real life cases on Court TV to the reality-based fiction on CSI and other network shows, there's almost always something to watch about some area of forensics. Although the television shows are usually based on real science, some aspects of criminal investigation are simplified or made a little more exciting for

Search It!
American Academy of Forensic Sciences at ***www.aafs.org*** and International Association for Identification at ***www.theiai.org***

Read It!
Young Forensic Scientists Forum newsletter at ***www.aafs.org/yfsf/index.htm*** and *Forensic Science Communications* at ***www.fbi.gov/hq/lab/fsc/current/index.htm***

Learn It!
- Bachelor's degree in forensic science
- Advanced degree in science or forensics

Earn It!
Median annual salary is $41,040. (Source: U.S. Department of Labor)

Find It!
Look for jobs at associations such as the American Society of Crime Laboratory Directors at ***www.ascld.org/employment.html*** or the International Association for Identification at ***www.theiai.org/jobs***.

Get Started Now!

- Take classes in the sciences, especially those that include a lot of laboratory work.
- Courtroom testimony is a critical part of the job for forensic technicians and forensic scientists. Those who cannot make an effective presentation to lawyers, judges, and juries are not valuable to any organization. Participate in student government, on debate teams, or in any other activity that will help you speak with clarity and confidence.
- Learn forensic science jargon. Check out the glossary from the Virginia Institute of Forensic Science and Medicine at ***www.vifsm.org/overview/glossary.html***.
- Get more information about ballistics science from FirearmsID at ***www.firearmsid.com***.
- For an explanation of how DNA typing works, check out The Why Files at ***www.whyfiles.org/126dna_forensic***.
- You can learn more about how polygraphs work from How Stuff Works at ***www.people.howstuffworks.com/lie-detector.htm***.

Hire Yourself!

You are the lead forensic investigator and have been called to the scene of an explosion at a railroad station. Many people have been killed or injured, and the train and station are in shambles. Using the FBI Handbook of Forensic Services at ***www.fbi.gov/hq/lab/handbook/intro.htm***, write an outline of how you would secure the crime scene to preserve the evidence and protect the safety of workers processing the scene, how you would organize and assign workers to search the scene for evidence, and what types of analysis you would expect to conduct.

the show to work. In real life, many more people are involved in investigating a crime, with each technician having his or her own specialty.

Forensic science technicians investigate crimes by collecting and analyzing physical evidence. Much of their work is done in laboratories, but they often go directly to the scene of a crime to find and protect potentially valuable evidence.

Forensic science technicians work with both physical evidence (things like weapons, clothing, or drugs) and trace evidence (less obvious things like fiber, hair, or tissue samples). Most forensic technicians specialize in a specific area of expertise.

Ballistics experts look at the bullets themselves, bullet paths, and gunshot residue to determine what weapon was used and how the crime occurred. Although investigators have used ballistics to help solve crimes for many years, today's science has made this specialty more complex and more accurate than ever.

Those who specialize in biochemistry analyze and classify biological fluids using DNA typing and other techniques. They may analyze foods and other materials found at crime scenes or search for drugs or poisons or possible drug interactions. They may examine fluid or tissue samples, trying to match the DNA to that of other samples, or work with evidence such as hair, fiber, wood, or soil, looking for clues about each element's source and composition. DNA testing is a relatively new science. It was first used in police work in 1986 and has become very common in recent years as its cost decreased and availability has increased. DNA testing is based on the idea that each person has a unique genetic "fingerprint" that is present in every cell of a person's body.

Sometimes forensic technicians find useful evidence from things that may no longer even exist. They may work with the impressions left by

teeth, tools, shoes, or tires. They may use the pattern of blood splatter or fingerprints found at a crime scene.

Other technicians specialize in the administration of polygraph, or "lie-detector" tests. Polygraph testing has long been controversial and is usually not acceptable as evidence in court. It is based on the assumption that people will have different physiological reactions when they are not telling the truth.

There are countless other areas of forensic technician specialties. There are forensic anthropologists, forensic entomologists, and forensic botanists, among others.

Although forensic technicians usually have a bachelor's degree, it is sometimes possible to get into the field through internships or starting at the very bottom of the laboratory ladder and learning on the job.

Forensic scientists, on the other hand, usually have master's degrees or even PhDs. A forensic scientist is an expert in chemistry, physics, biology, toxicology, or some other field. While forensic scientists may also collect, sort, and preserve evidence, their primary job is to perform the scientific analysis of it.

Forensic technicians and scientists perform their work in laboratories, at crime scenes, in offices, and in morgues. They may work for federal, state, or local government, forensic laboratories, hospitals, universities, toxicology laboratories, police departments, medical examiner and coroner offices, or as independent forensic science consultants. Critical skills for forensic technicians and scientists include curiosity, the ability to look at things in different ways to solve problems, excellent public speaking skills, and a strong stomach for crime scenes.

find your future

hazardous materials technician

hazardous materials technician

hazardous materials technician Hazardous materials (HAZMAT) technicians are specialists who are called in to contain and remove chemicals and other types of materials that pose a danger to people or the environment. This has become necesscary because over the years, many construction and manufacturing materials and processes once considered harmless and effective have been found to be very harmful. For example, at one time lead was added to paint to make it last longer. Then we discovered that this paint can cause lead poisoning when it ages and crumbles from walls, a problem that particularly affects children who may put the chips in their mouths in addition to breathing lead dust in the air.

In addition, asbestos, a fiber that was used extensively for fireproofing and insulation, is now known to cause cancer or other lung disease when its dust escapes from walls as older buildings are torn down or renovated. Nuclear energy and other modern industrial processes result in a variety of dangerous waste products. And we now know that some types of mold found in heating and air-conditioning ducts, within walls,

Get Started Now!

- Take courses in science and math to help understand and mitigate the risks of hazardous contaminants.
- Become familiar with HAZMAT lingo at the Agency for Toxic Substances and Disease Registry (ATSDR) at ***www.atsdr.cdc.gov/glossary.html***.
- Catch up on local and national HAZMAT news at the U.S. Chemical Safety and Hazard Investigation Board's website, ***www.csb.gov***.

Search It!
United States National Response Team at ***www.nrt.org***

Read It!
HazMat Management magazine at ***www.hazmatmag.com***

Learn It!
- Minimum of high school diploma or GED
- On-the-job training, plus formal training for some specialties
- Find classes at the North American Hazardous Materials Management Association at ***www.nahmma.org/training***

Earn It!
Median annual salary is $32,460. (Source: U.S. Department of Labor)

Find It!
Find job leads at the Dangerous Goods Advisory Council at ***www.dgac.org/jobs.htm***.

Hire Yourself!

You are a HAZMAT worker responding to an overturned tanker truck that was carrying 5,000 gallons of bleach. Bleach can release chlorine gas, a dangerous toxin and environmental contaminant. Use the Internet to research the effects of chlorine gas, as well as containment and cleanup strategies. You might want to start by using your favorite Internet search engine like Google or Yahoo to run a search for "chlorine gas containment."

If the cloud of chlorine gas is spreading from the truck at a rate of three miles every 20 minutes, how long until homes within a five-mile radius are affected? If the wind picks up and causes the spread to double in speed, how soon will homes in a 20-mile radius have to evacuate?

and in attics and basements can cause such severe allergic reactions that extensive efforts must be taken to remove it safely.

The duties of HAZMAT workers and the tools they use depend on the type and threat level of materials they work with. For example, asbestos abatement workers may wear disposable or reusable coveralls, gloves, goggles, and a respirator to protect their lungs from airborne particles. They may use tools as simple as a broom, or as complex as a highly efficient vacuum cleaner that traps asbestos and stores it in a secure container.

In cases of nuclear, biological, or chemical hazards released by accident or in a terrorist attack, HAZMAT workers could be required to wear special containment suits in the contaminated zone. Although the suits may look like they belong on astronauts, they completely prevent any dangerous materials from touching the worker.

After hazardous materials are collected and contained, specialized HAZMAT workers prepare the materials for treatment, transportation, and storage. Laws require these workers to be able to verify shipping manifests (records of what is being transported) to ensure that dangerous materials receive the proper treatment. Hazardous materials are rarely stored near where they are produced, so they often end up at incinerators or landfills in remote locations. HAZMAT workers at these facilities assess materials, organize and track their whereabouts, and prepare them for storage or destruction.

Being a HAZMAT worker can be a stressful and uncomfortable job. To ease the stress and minimize the danger that workers undergo, most teams operate under highly regimented circumstances using plans developed weeks or even years ahead of time. Even when workers respond to an emergency situation, crews and supervisors take every precaution to ensure that the worksite is safe. Staying calm and being able to work as a team helps crew members stay out of danger.

HAZMAT workers must have at least a high school diploma or a GED. They learn skills particular to their individual roles on the job and must pass licensing exams to work with different materials. Some specialties also require a 32- to 40-hour training course; nuclear HAZMAT workers need an additional three months of classes. HAZMAT workers also take yearly refresher courses to keep their licenses up to date. Many HAZMAT workers get licensed to work with more than one material for more flexibility on the job.

HAZMAT workers are employed by waste management and remediation services, specialty contractors, and government agencies. The field has grown considerably in recent years, reflecting an increased concern for a safe and clean environment. HAZMAT workers are less affected than other workers by fluctuations in the economy because HAZMAT facilities must operate regardless of the state of the economy, so job security can be exceedingly high for those who choose to stay in the field.

Search It!
The American Society for the Prevention of Cruelty to Animals at ***www.aspca.org***

Read It!
The Humane Society University news on-line at ***www.hsus2.org/hsu/whatsnew1.html***

Learn It!

- High school diploma or GED required for entry-level positions
- Completion of peace officer and firearms training courses

Earn It!
Median annual salary is $25,980. (Source: U.S. Department of Labor)

Find It!
Humane law enforcement (HLE) officers work for local animal control agencies. Find local agencies at ***www.aspca.org*** and at the National Animal Control Association at ***www.nacanet.org***.

humane law enforcement officer

Humane law enforcement officers (also known as animal control officers or animal "cops") are a special breed of hero who protect animals from people and people from animals. Animals are abused and neglected every day. One job of humane law enforcement officers is to step in and put a stop to it. On the other hand, when wild animals such as moose, deer, or coyotes get a little too close to human habitats for comfort, they are responsible for relocating animals into natural, safer environments.

Animal cruelty is the term used to describe the crime of intentional conduct that results in the harm or suffering of an animal or the willful neglect of an animal. Neglect includes the failure to provide the food, water, or medical care that a given animal needs. Both acts are illegal and sufficient cause for the intervention of a humane law enforcement officer.

Animal cops have numerous responsibilities. They investigate reports of alleged abuse and neglect and, when necessary, remove stray, uncontrolled, or abused animals to more stable conditions. Animal cops also examine maltreated animals and arrange for medical treatment as appro-

Get Started Now!

Use these strategies to get ready for a future as a humane law enforcement officer:

- Check out industry information and opportunities by visiting World Animal Net at ***www.worldanimal.net***.
- Classes in science, biology, zoology, health, and psychology may come in handy.
- Volunteer at a local animal shelter.

Hire Yourself!

Visit the International Fund for Animal Welfare at ***www.ifaw.org***. Research specific instances of animal cruelty and violations described on the site. Then draft a bill of rights for animals. Remember to consider all animals: domestic, farm, marine, endangered wildlife, etc. Sympathizing with the plight of animals will prepare you for a career protecting their rights!

priate. They investigate reports of animal attacks, interview witnesses, and prepare reports of activities and cases.

Another important function involves public education about the proper treatment of animals. This might involve school presentations, booths at public events, and even, in some cases, one-on-one instruction in the care and feeding of animals. In the long run, these efforts make their jobs easier, not to mention less heartbreaking.

When they are not investigating reports of animal cruelty, animal control officers may patrol streets for stray animals. If an animal is found and is healthy, it is impounded. If it is injured or ill, it may be taken to an animal hospital, or "put down" (euthanized) if its condition is too serious to be treated.

In most cases, human law enforcement officers work fairly normal hours. However, those working for shelters in small communities with fewer employees may be on-call around the clock or work more than the usual 40 hours a week.

Animal cops run many of the same risks that regular police officers do. Thus, it is imperative that they know how to handle dangerous situations. Some pet owners are unpleasantly surprised to find that harming an animal is a crime, and their reactions can be unpredictable.

The minimum requirement for becoming a humane law enforcement officer is completion of high school, or a GED. Initial and ongoing training is also part of the deal. Initial training might include standard peace officer training and weapon-handling instruction. Examples of ongoing training include chemical capture, euthanasia, and National Animal Control Association certification. A college degree in a related subject, such as criminal justice or veterinary medicine, is helpful and certainly gives a candidate the advantage over one without similar qualifications. Humane law enforcement officers may also work in other areas of the animal control profession, which includes public health and safety, and law enforcement.

Search It!
U.S. Citizenship and Immigration Services (USCIS) at ***http://uscis.gov/graphics/index.htm***

Read It!
News in immigration at ***http://uscis.gov/graphics/whatsnew.htm***

Learn It!
- High school diploma
- Successful completion of one to two and a half months of specialized training

Earn It!
Starting base annual salary ranges from $24,075 to $38,767 (per GS-5 through GS-7 designations on the federal employee pay schedule).
(Source: U.S. Office of Personnel Management)

Find It!
Apply on-line at the U.S. Immigration and Customs Services, at ***http://uscis.gov/graphics/workfor/careers/vacancy.htm***.

immigration officer

Since the first wave of immigrants arrived on the Mayflower in 1620, the United States has been a country of immigrants. Historically, America has always been seen as a refuge against persecution, poor economic conditions, and government instability. This keeps U.S. immigration a hot topic, and relevant policies and enforcement are constantly under discussion. Today, more than 9 percent of the U.S. population is foreign-born, and 250,000 to 350,000 new immigrants are admitted each year. Our government employs immigration officers to facilitate the immigration process.

Immigration officers function in several different capacities. Adjudication officers review immigrations applications submitted from virtually every corner of the world for virtually every reason under the sun. These officers must carefully screen each application and determine which are granted and which are not. Applications may range from a business requesting permission to import foreign workers to a U.S. citizen requesting permission for a foreign-born relative to immigrate. The

Get Started Now!

Here are some strategies to consider on a path to a career in immigration:

- Take as many computer, psychology, and language classes as you can.
- You'll need good communication and interpersonal skills. Try being a peer mediator.
- You'll need to be familiar with different areas of the world and the conditions in each area that may cause people to apply for asylum. Take classes in modern world history and current events.

Hire Yourself!

You have been hired by USCIS to review asylum applications. Go to the USCIS home page at ***www.uscis.gov*** and look up the Immigration and Nationality Act. What conditions qualify? Write a short report on your findings and include any current events in the news that may constitute a situation in which a foreign citizen might qualify for asylum in the United States.

review process usually involves interviewing applicants, performing background checks, and conducting other investigations in order to detect possible fraud.

Some immigrants come here seeking asylum, which is special permission granted on humanitarian grounds when it is not safe for a person to remain in or return to his or her home country. Immigration asylum officers determine whether or not the applicant's circumstances qualify under the Immigration and Nationality Act, and whether that person deserves to be granted asylum. Applicants for asylum must show that they were persecuted or have a well-founded fear of persecution on account of race, religion, nationality, political opinion, or membership in a particular social group.

Asylum officers must be able to work well under pressure, as time is of the essence in the cases of those truly needing asylum. But they must also have a firm grasp of human psychology and the ability to judge character well since some pleas are purposely misrepresented.

Finally, immigration information officers explain what benefits may be received under the immigration and nationality laws, and assist in the application procedure. They know what forms need to be filled out for each type of request, and can estimate the waiting period applicants should expect while their applications are being reviewed. Immigration information officers serve as a kind of "go-between" between the government and the applicant.

To become an immigration officer, applicants must be between 21 and 37 years old at the time of appointment. They must also be a U.S. citizen with at least a high school education. College training in a related field like political science, criminology, or foreign language often provides an advantage over other applicants.

Immigration officers play an important role in safeguarding national security. In fact, this role is so important that, in 2003, the former Immigration and Naturalization Service became part of the Department of Homeland Security. Character and background checks are now

essential. That means that all applicants might be asked to take lie detector and personality tests, be interviewed by a psychologist, consent to having family and friends interviewed, and take a drug test.

Applicants must also complete a training program that can last one to two and a half months, depending on the specific job. For adjudication officers, the basic training course lasts one month and covers areas such as immigration law, adjudication process and procedures, naturalization process and procedures, and fraudulent document detection, among others. Training for asylum officers lasts about two and a half months and consists of two parts. Part one covers the same topics covered in adjudication officer training. Part two is a five-week asylum-specific course and covers topics such as U.S. asylum and refugee law, international human rights law, and effective country conditions research. Immigration information officer training is one month long and covers topics such as immigration law, immigration officer duties and responsibilities, fraudulent document detection, and customer service.

find
information systems
security specialist
your future

information systems security specialist

Sometimes it seems like people spend half their lives in front of a computer. Correspondence via e-mail has almost entirely replaced "snail mail." People use the Internet to buy everything from golf clubs to grapes. Even companies share vast amounts of information and conduct much of their business on-line. This surge of electronic communication has created the need for information systems security specialists.

Information systems security specialists are responsible for planning, coordinating, and installing methods and programs to protect an organization's information. These specialists may educate users about computer security measures already in place (such as spam filters in e-mail software) or they might install security software. Some may monitor networks for security violations while others investigate potential cyber crime.

Have you ever used a credit card to purchase something on-line? The reason you can do so without worrying about someone stealing your

Get Started Now!

Use these strategies to get ready for a future in information technology:

- Check out certification options at ***http://sageweb.sage.org/cert***.
- Math is essential—data encryption is, in essence, a mathematical language. So—you guessed it! Take as many math classes as you can.
- Get a head start and take a computer science class at a community college, if your schedule allows.

Search It!

Association of Computer Support Specialists at ***www.acss.org***

Read It!

Information Security magazine at ***http://infosecuritymag.techtarget.com***

Learn It!

- Associate's degree in computer-related field
- Bachelor's degree suggested in computer science or information systems
- Certification in specific computer programs
- Relevant work experience

Earn It!

Median annual salary is $42,320. (Source: U.S. Department of Labor)

Find It!

Information systems security specialists work for private companies, computer systems design consultants, banks, and government agencies. Find jobs by applying directly to the company or search sites like ***www.acss.org***.

credit card number and using it to buy thousands of dollars of merchandise is because special measures have been taken to secure this sensitive information. The same goes for school records, tax information, a company's sales figures, or top-secret government intelligence.

Information security specialists do this in a number of ways. They encrypt (use complex mathematical languages to disguise) data transmission. They install firewalls to hide confidential information and filter corrupted information transfers. They may also change individual users' access methods if unauthorized access to information has occurred. Specialists also conduct periodic tests to make sure security measures already in place are working properly.

Computer security specialists often work "in-house," meaning they work within a company, ready to correct whatever problems or breaches may arise. However, it is becoming more common for specialists to do their work remotely, using laptops, modems, and e-mail to respond to user/client needs.

There is no single path to becoming an information systems security specialist. With the need for specialists increasing with remarkable speed, new ways of entering the field are opening up. At one time it was imperative for specialists to have a college degree in a related field. Today it is becoming common for employers to accept various certifications and professional, on-the-job experience in its place.

Information systems security specialists should have strong analytical skills and problem-solving abilities. They should also be comfortable communicating with others since they'll spend a good deal of time educating users on security measures and responding to client needs and problems. Those who enter this field should be ready to commit to a lot of continuing education. Information systems security specialists must work hard to keep abreast of technological advancements, and are often

Hire Yourself

You need to encrypt data in a user's file. Go to your local paper, and cut out the first two sentences in one of the top stories. Then, use a numerical language to encode the sentences. For instance, assign each letter of the alphabet a number, and rewrite the sentences numerically. Or, if you want to get sophisticated, use a simple equation to rewrite the sentences. Then, show your new "sentences" to a friend or teacher, explain your process, and see if he or she can decode the information.

asked—if not required—by employers to take courses to keep their skills current.

With the technology boom in recent years (believe it or not, there was an era when the Internet did not exist!), the growth in jobs for computer specialists has been huge. In 2002, computer support specialists and administrators held about 758,000 jobs. Demand may slow down a bit over the next few years, as some jobs are outsourced to workers in other countries, but overall demand is still expected to increase faster than the average for all other occupations.

Search It!

National Society of Professional Insurance Investigators at ***www.nspii.com***

Read It!

Insurance Journal at ***www.insurancejournal.com*** and *Claims* magazine at ***www.claimsmag.com***

Learn It!

- College degree with a focus on general studies majors
- Experience in law enforcement or claims adjustment
- Licensing required in many states

Earn It!

Median annual salary is $43,020. (Source: U.S. Department of Labor)

Find It!

Insurance investigators work for special investigative units of insurance companies and as independent investigators. Potential employers include USAA at ***www.usaa.com*** and Allstate at ***www.allstate.com***.

insurance investigator

Insurance is basically a way for many people to share a financial risk, with everyone paying a little so that protection is affordable for all. People buy insurance for their automobiles, homes, businesses, health, and even for their lives.

When people exaggerate or make up claims (or reports) for things that they have insured in order to get money that they are not entitled to, they are committing the crime of fraud. The job of insurance investigators is to look into all kinds of claims to see which are authentic and which involve fraud. To do this, the investigators use a combination of very sophisticated methods and some good old-fashioned detective work.

Suppose your school has 200 seniors, one gown is lost or stolen at graduation every year, and it costs $200 to replace that gown. The class may decide that each senior will put in $1 in advance so no one person risks having to come up with $200. If your gown ends up being the missing one, the $200 that was collected pays for it, and you save $199. If your gown is not missing, you only paid $1 for some peace of mind.

Get Started Now!

- Learn all you can about the insurance industry and different types of insurance.
- Learn about some of the most outrageous, as well as the most common, forms of insurance fraud. Check out the Insurance Fraud Hall of Shame from the Coalition Against Insurance Fraud at ***www.insurancefraud.org***.
- Participate in clubs, student government, and other situations to hone leadership and communication skills.

Hire Yourself!

You are a self-employed insurance investigator. Your business has grown so much that you are ready to hire more investigators. Research ways to find insurance fraud, including the articles at ***www.pimall.com/nais/insrec.html***, and prepare a list of warning signs that your new investigators should look for when investigating suspicious claims.

Simple, right? But what if two additional students decide to keep their gowns and report them "stolen." Now the group has to come up with $600 (the cost of three gowns), and each of the 200 seniors has to contribute $3 instead of $1. Apply this principle to major real life situations like health and property and it's easy to see how costs can quickly skyrocket when fraud enters the picture.

Most insurance fraud involves auto, health, or catastrophe insurance. Experts estimate that one third of all claims for injury in car accidents involve some amount of fraud. Some people exaggerate injuries to themselves or to their vehicles with the intention of getting more money from their insurance companies. They may be helped by doctors or auto body workers who write false reports and share the extra money. In some cases, organized rings of criminals "stage" accidents to bilk innocent victims and their insurance companies out of exorbitant sums of money.

In the area of health insurance, it has been estimated that fraud costs Americans as much as $80 to $95 billion each year! This fraud might range from medical providers submitting bills for unnecessary services or for services never provided to employees lying about physical ailments so they can be compensated for staying home from work. Even in the face of horrible disasters, some people have tried to "cash in" through insurance fraud. After hurricanes and other disasters, some people claim the loss of expensive property that they never owned in the first place. Victims of house fires or burglaries have been known to claim that jewelry and other valuables that never existed were taken. Some unscrupulous people actually have claimed that spouses died in the September 11 attacks in an attempt to collect insurance settlements.

Insurance investigators do a lot of their work through the Internet and on the telephone. They review medical and financial records, examine damage, and look for patterns of claims involving the same claimants. They also work outside of the office doing surveillance, interviewing witnesses, and checking on claims.

Search It!
The Federal Judicial Center at *www.fjc.gov* and The Federal Judiciary at *www.uscourts.gov*

Read It!
Benchmark at *http://aja.ncsc.dni.us/benchmk/Benchmark.html* and *Court Review* at *http://aja.ncsc.dni.us/courtrv/review.html*

Learn It!
- Minimum requirement for a judgeship is a bachelor's degree and work experience
- Most judges have a law degree

Earn It!
Median annual salary is $94,100. (Source: U.S. Department of Labor)

Find It!
Judges are either elected or appointed to their positions. Most have extensive experience as attorneys before assuming judicial responsibilities. For information see *www.uscourts.gov*.

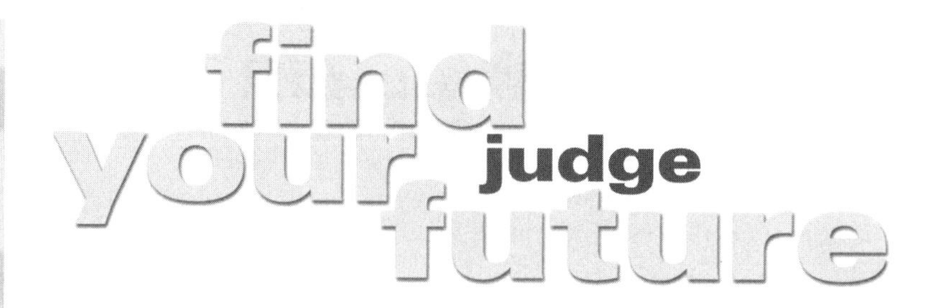

judge

Judges are essential to our legal system. They impact every part of our society, dispensing justice in cases involving seemingly minor infractions of the law such as people cited for running a red light, and in major legal issues like equal access to public education.

We usually think of judges as presiding over courtroom trials, and that certainly is a big part of some judges' jobs. During a courtroom trial, a judge has five major responsibilities:

- to ensure that order is maintained and laws are followed
- to rule whether the evidence is admissible in court
- to instruct juries about applicable law and to explain standards for reaching a verdict
- to sentence convicted criminal defendants
- and, in bench trials where there is no jury, to evaluate evidence and determine the outcome of cases

Some of the other responsibilities of judges include duties such as awarding compensation for damages, conducting preliminary hearings to determine probable cause for holding defendants over for trial, set-

Get Started Now!

- Learn more about how trials work. A good place to start is at the American Bar Association website at *www.abanet.org/publiced/courts/trialsteps.html*.
- Visit a court in your area. Make a list of some of the ways the judge keeps the trial moving along smoothly.
- Immerse yourself in history and the political process by taking courses in these subject areas.
- Participate in mock trials, local elections, and other opportunities to get a firsthand look at our political process in action.

Hire Yourself!

Use resources you find at the American Bar Association's public education website at ***www.abanet.org/publiced/courts/home.html*** to create a chart describing how courts work.

tling disputes between opposing attorneys, and writing decisions on cases. Some judges are responsible for matters pertaining to families, such as granting divorces and dividing assets between spouses, ruling on custody and access disputes, and enforcing court orders regarding custody and support of children. Some even perform wedding ceremonies. Other responsibilities often assigned to judges are supervising other judges, court officers, and the court's administrative staff.

Judges are either elected or appointed to their positions. Some appointments, as is the case for U.S. Supreme Court Justices, are for life. In situations where judges are elected, assignments are for a fixed but renewable term that ranges between four and 14 years, depending on the location. Judges are also elected or appointed to a specific type of court, such as appeals court or family court.

There are three levels of courts: federal, state, and municipal courts. Where a case is tried usually depends on the issue at hand. The authority of federal courts is limited to specific types of cases. Federal courts were originally established to decide disputes involving the Constitution and laws passed by Congress. Today federal courts hear cases in which the United States is either a plaintiff or a defendant; cases involving violations of the Constitution or federal laws; cases between citizens of different states (if an amount of money concerned is over $75,000); and cases involving bankruptcy, copyright, patent, and maritime law.

State and local courts are more involved with the concerns (and crimes) of individual citizens. The distinction can be tricky. Robbery is a crime defined by state laws, except that robbing a bank whose deposits are insured by a federal agency is a federal crime. Using or selling drugs is a state

crime, but bringing drugs into the country or across state lines is a federal crime.

Within both the federal and state court systems, there are two more types of courts: trial courts and appellate courts. Trial courts review the facts and resolve disputes. Appellate courts determine whether the law was applied appropriately in a trial. Courts are also separated into civil and criminal courts, depending on the content of their cases. A civil case involves a plaintiff (a person, corporation, or government) who claims that the defendant (another person, corporation, or government) has failed to carry out a legal duty owed to the plaintiff. A criminal case, on the other hand, involves a defendant (the person accused of committing the crime), but the victim does not have to be the plaintiff. Instead, district attorneys prosecute cases on behalf of the people under their jurisdiction.

Regardless of these distinctions, all courts rely on ethical, legally sound judges doing their jobs day after day, case after case.

lawyer According to the *Occupational Outlook Handbook*, lawyers, also called attorneys, act as both advocates and advisors in our society. As advocates, they represent one of the opposing sides in criminal and civil trials by presenting evidence and arguing in court to support their client. As advisors, lawyers counsel their clients concerning their legal rights and obligations and suggest particular courses of action in business and personal matters. Whether acting as an advocate or an advisor, all attorneys must be adept at applying the intent of laws and judicial decisions to the specific circumstances faced by their client.

All lawyers specialize in certain types of law. In general, law is divided into two categories: criminal and civil. Criminal law has to do with enforcing the laws that protect people and property. In a criminal law case, charges are brought against suspected wrongdoers by the state or federal government (the prosecution). The defendant is the person

Get Started Now!

- Take classes in government and business law. Pay special attention to how our laws have changed or not changed over time.
- Learn more about different legal specializations from the American Bar Association at ***www.abanet.org/careercounsel/profile/profession.html***.
- Learn about how trials work. Visit a courtroom to watch a trial. Follow a murder trial from start to finish at ***http://library.thinkquest.org/2760/table.htm***. Or get more details on criminal and civil trials from How Lawsuits Work at ***http://people.howstuffworks.com/lawsuit.htm***.
- Try to get a summer or part-time job at a law firm. You will not be able to see confidential information about clients, but any job will help you learn more about what lawyers do.

Search It!
American Bar Association at ***www.abanet.org*** and Law and Policy Institutions Guide at ***www.lpig.org***

Read It!
Find links to law-related resources at the Law Library of Congress at ***www.loc.gov/law/guide*** and the 'Lectric Law Library at ***www.lectlaw.com***

Learn It!
- Four-year college degree
- Three years in law school
- Successful completion of state bar exam

Earn It!
Median annual salary is $90,290. (Source: U.S. Department of Labor)

Find It!
Look for jobs through state and local bar associations. Find their websites at ***www.abanet.org/careercounsel/statebar.html***.

Hire Yourself!

You have been hired as a lawyer to review your school's student handbook. Obtain a copy from the school office and read it carefully to identify any regulations that might be questionable in terms of student or teacher rights. Write a mock legal brief describing the rule, potential problems, and suggested solutions.

who is charged with a crime. Criminal lawyers specialize in one of these two sides. For obvious reasons, it's important for attorneys to be well spoken, knowledgeable about relevant laws, and able to think quickly on their feet. It's also critical for them to know the rules of evidence and other procedures of criminal courtrooms.

If you've ever seen lawyers featured on a television show or movie, you've probably seen glamorized examples of criminal lawyers. Of course, in real life, for every minute a lawyer spends pontificating in court, they spend hours (and sometimes hundreds of hours) in preparation. Preparing for a criminal trial involves interviewing witnesses, researching similar cases, writing and filing motions and countermotions, and so on.

Civil cases are disagreements between people or organizations in which one party has asked the court to intervene. Civil cases can be about divorce, child custody, contracts, intellectual property (copyrights and patents), and product liability.

Other legal work is totally unrelated to trials. Lawyers can help people with real estate transactions, making sure that everything is done according to local property laws. They write wills for people and serve as the executor of the will after that person's death. Other lawyers work in financial areas (such as tax law or bankruptcy proceedings), adoption law, or contract law.

Lawyers who work for businesses are often responsible for preventive action. They make sure that the business follows all laws regarding environmental compliance, non-discrimination, truthful advertising, safety testing, packaging requirements, and labor laws.

About three-quarters of all lawyers work in private practice—either for themselves or for a law firm. Private practice lawyers select their clients from people and organizations that want to hire them. Some lawyers work solely for one corporation, doing whatever that company needs in connection with running its business. Lawyers in that situation are generally called "house counsel." Many lawyers work for the government. In addition to helping the government prosecute criminal cases, lawyers are needed to help develop federal and state programs, to draft and interpret laws and legislation, and to establish procedures to enforce new and existing laws.

Because lawyers are so important to every aspect of our lives, they are held to a higher standard of ethics than most other professions. The Multistate Professional Responsibility Examination (MPRE), which tests law students' knowledge of legal ethics, professional responsibility, and judicial conduct, is now required in many states.

The need for different specialties in the law has changed over time and will probably continue to do so. The aging of our population has created a need for lawyers well versed in geriatric law. The advent of the Internet and file sharing has created a market for lawyers trained in intellectual property law. There will always be a demand for lawyers. However, if the desire to enter this field continues to remain strong, competition for acceptance to law schools and for jobs in the field will become even stronger than it is today.

Search It!
American Association of Legal Nurse Consultants at ***www.aalnc.org***

Read It!
Nursing Spectrum Online at ***www.nursingspectrum.com***

Learn It!
- Must be a registered nurse
- Minimum of bachelor's degree in nursing

Earn It!
Independent legal nurse consultants earn between $70 and $200 an hour.
(Source: American Association of Legal Nurse Consultants)

Find It!
Legal nurse consultants work as employees or consultants for law firms, insurance companies, HMOs, and government agencies. Find job leads at sites like ***http://jobsearch.nursingworld.monster.com***.

legal nurse consultant

Registered nurses work at the heart of most routine medical care. So, it might come as no surprise that when lawyers need an expert opinion on medical issues, they often consult with a nurse. Legal nurse consultants combine years of nursing experience with basic legal knowledge to help attorneys and their clients understand health care issues. They help lawyers and their clients evaluate and try malpractice, personal injury, product liability, and other kinds of cases.

Nurse consultants perform many tasks for attorneys. At the beginning of a case, legal nurses work with the medical charts, records, and other notes. They may summarize pertinent information or organize the information in a way that makes a case easier to understand. Since nurses work with this type of information all the time, they are better able to

Get Started Now!

To secure your career as a legal nurse consultant, start now by doing the following:

- Take classes in biology, chemistry, and other sciences.
- Start learning about some of the current legal issues in medicine. Scan the Internet for cases on malpractice, product liability, and other related issues.
- Work on your research skills. Take classes that require you to do independent research and summarize other people's research.
- Take classes in speech and communication. Do projects that require you to explain something as an expert to people who know nothing about your topic.

Hire Yourself!

You are an attorney working on a medical malpractice lawsuit and need the expertise of a qualified legal nurse consultant. Use the resources you find at the 'Lectric Law Library Lawcopedia's forum on law and medicine at ***www.lectlaw.com/tmed.html*** to come up with a list of 10 interview questions to help you identify a qualified legal nurse consultant.

understand the information and more likely to notice things that are out of the ordinary. Legal nurses can also quickly identify things that may be missing from the notes, such as tests that should have been run, or patient visits that should have been conducted. Legal nurses are also able to quickly translate the abbreviations that are commonly used in medical notes—a much-appreciated skill among those unfamiliar with medical terminology.

In many legal situations, the core question is whether or not the patient received the "accepted level" of care. In order to determine exactly what that would include for the case in question, legal nurses often have to research a patient's condition or care by reviewing other medical literature or scientific studies. They may also consult with physicians and other health care providers. A legal nurse's evaluation of the patient's care often helps a lawyer decide whether a case has enough merit to go to trial.

For cases that do go to trial, legal nurses may testify as expert witnesses. They may also be asked to find and evaluate other experts to testify on a client's behalf. Nurses often serve as liaisons between the attorney, clients, and expert witnesses. They help witnesses prepare for the trial by participating in mock trials or developing trial exhibits. They also help attorneys prepare questions for expert witnesses from the opposing side.

Many legal nurse consultants are employed full time by a law office or insurance company, while others take on a series of short-term assignments for different companies. Many work independently, taking consulting jobs when they are available. Some independents keep their regular nursing jobs and accept consulting assignments on more of a freelance basis.

At least three to five years of nursing experience and a basic understanding of the law are mandatory for this job. Good organization skills can help legal nurse consultants juggle duties when they work with more than one attorney or on different aspects of a case. Excellent

communication skills are important for explaining complex medical issues to lawyers, clients, and other expert witnesses. If a legal nurse consultant works independently, understanding small business law can help keep his or her work running smoothly.

All legal nurse consultants are registered nurses with at least a bachelor's degree from a four-year college or university and a state license to practice nursing from the state. Many gain specific knowledge of medical law on the job while working with attorneys. A few four-year universities, community colleges, and distance-learning companies offer certificate programs in legal nurse consulting, with a concentration on basic law and the specifics of running a small business.

With medical lawsuits increasing in frequency, the demand for good legal nurse consultants is growing. Recessions are unlikely to put a damper on business in this field.

municipal firefighter

It's quite possible that becoming a firefighter is one of the most common career aspirations of young children. Just one visit to the local firehouse—big red trucks, shiny black boots, clanging bells, and all—makes an indelible impression on many a young mind. They instinctively know that firefighting is an exciting, important job.

However, turning those childhood fantasies into adult realities takes an incredible amount of work. Before someone can even be considered to try out for a firefighter position, they must pass a battery of tests. First there is a written test that covers math, reading, and general knowledge. If they pass that test, they go on to tests of strength, physical stamina, coordination, and agility. Finally, there's a medical examination that includes drug screening. If they pass on all of these, they just might be considered as a candidate for firefighter training. Even those who make

Get Started Now!

- Before you can even begin firefighter training, you'll have to pass a general civil service test that includes math, reading, science, and general knowledge. Make sure you have a firm foundation in all of your basic subjects.
- Participate in activities that require teamwork, such as team sports, or the school newspaper.
- Learn some vocabulary used by firefighters at ***www.riotacts.com/fire/glossary.html***.
- See how much you already know about firefighting. Take the Firefighting Quiz from American-Firefighter.com at ***www.american-firefighter.com/quiz***.

Search It!

U.S. Fire Administration at ***www.usfa.fema.gov*** and Firehouse.Com at ***www.firehouse.com***

Read It!

Fire Engineering magazine at ***http://fe.pennnet.com***, *Fire Command and Control Foundation* magazine at ***http://firecommandandcontrol.com***, and *FireRescue* magazine at ***www.jems.com/firerescue***

Learn It!

- High school diploma or GED
- Fire academy training
- Community college courses in fire science are a definite plus

Earn It!

Median annual salary is $36,230. (Source: U.S. Department of Labor)

Find It!

Check with your local fire department or look at current job postings at ***www.firehouse.com***.

Hire Yourself!

You have been assigned to go to an elementary school to teach the children about your profession. Make a display that shows different types of firefighting and rescue equipment (including protective clothing, axes, chain saws, fire extinguishers, ladders, and the different types of fire trucks). Prepare a simple description of each piece of equipment, along with an explanation of how or why it is used. Hint: You can learn about the protective clothing worn by municipal firefighters at ***www.ci.davis.ca.us/fire/pct***. Learn about fire engines at ***www.ci.davis.ca.us/fire/tour*** and at ***www.howstuffworks.com/fire-engine.htm***.

it as a firefighter eventually face many of these same tests over and over throughout their careers.

Each state has different procedures for training and selecting firefighters. In most, a candidate goes to one of the state's fire training academies for several weeks for classes and practical training. There they study subjects that include firefighting techniques and equipment, hazardous materials control, local building codes, emergency medical procedures, and fire prevention and safety. The courses may include math, chemistry, and building construction. Those that meet these challenges may be assigned to a fire company as a probationary firefighter to start on-the-job training under the supervision of experienced firefighters. Probationary status may last for several years, with frequent practical and written tests. During that time new firefighters learn more about fighting fires, as well as how to drive and operate fire trucks. Some fire departments even test your knowledge of the streets in the city.

In addition to having the physical abilities required for the job and passing all of the technical tests, successful firefighters have certain personality traits. Good interpersonal skills are critical. Firefighting is a team effort and, as in many team sports, success is not achieved by any one individual's performance. Flexibility is another important skill for firefighters. During the course of one fire, you may have to assume responsibility for several different jobs.

In many areas, firefighters are expected to work 50 hours a week or more. Schedules rarely follow traditional nine to five patterns. Instead, it is not unusual for squads of firefighters to be on duty at the fire station for 24 to 72 hours in a row, rotating two or three days on and two or three days off with other squads. Of course, these extended shifts include time for sleeping and eating. However, firefighters must be ready to respond to emergencies whether they happen at 3:00 P.M. or at 3:00 A.M. Other firefighters alternate stints of day shifts and night shifts.

Firefighters do much more than put out fires and rescue people. At the scene of the fire, they also provide emergency medical attention as needed, ventilate smoke-filled areas, and attempt to salvage the contents of buildings. They may remain at the site of a disaster long after the fire is out, making sure it does not recur and rescuing trapped survivors.

About half of all fire departments also provide ambulance services. In fact, in many areas, firefighters respond to more medical emergencies than they do to fires.

When not responding to emergencies, firefighters clean and maintain equipment, conduct practice drills and fire inspections, and participate in physical fitness activities. They also prepare written reports on fire incidents and review fire science literature to keep abreast of technological developments and changing administrative practices and policies.

occupational health and safety specialist

Sometimes earning a living can be downright dangerous. Machines can cause injury when parts become worn or broken. Unpleasant or toxic fumes or chemicals may be released. Repetitive use of seemingly harmless equipment can cause physical injury over time. (Think about carpal tunnel problems in people who work at a keyboard all day). Even in work situations that do not present any specific or obvious concerns, there is always a risk of slips, falls, fires, or pollution.

To minimize dangers for their employees, companies frequently hire occupational health and safety specialists to inspect and improve job sites. These specialists are specifically trained to develop safer, healthier, and more efficient ways of working. They also help employers follow federal and local laws that prevent harm to workers, property, the environment, and the general public.

The field of occupational safety and health encompasses several different professions. Specialists may work in specific niches that include

Search It!
American Industrial Hygiene Association at ***www.aiha.gov***, The National Institute for Occupational Safety and Health (NIOSH) at ***www.cdc.gov/niosh***, and Occupational Safety and Health Administration (OSHA) at ***www.osha.gov***

Read It!
Occupational Health and Safety magazine at ***www.ohsonline.com***

Learn It!
- Usually a minimum of a four-year college degree in safety or a related field
- Extensive on-the-job training

Earn It!
Median annual salary is $46,010. (Source: U.S. Department of Labor)

Find It!
Look for job leads at the U.S. Department of Labor's Occupational Safety and Health Administration at ***www.osha.gov***.

Get Started Now!

- Take courses in English, math, biology, chemistry, and physics.
- Read up on the government's standards for health and safety in OSHA's Technical Manual at ***www.osha.gov/dts/osta/otm/otm_toc.html***.
- Find out what health and safety standards affect your parents' or teachers' workplaces.

Hire Yourself!

You are the occupational health and safety specialist for your school. Explore the different types of classrooms in the school, looking for possible health and safety problems. Is there mold or asbestos? Are there chemicals or equipment that could be dangerous? Does the cafeteria meet food handling safety regulations? Get ideas for other things to look for from the Environmental Protection Agency's Healthy School Environments website at ***http://cfpub.epa.gov/schools***. Prepare a presentation of your findings and your recommendations to improve health and safety in your school.

safety inspectors, industrial hygienists, environmental protection officers, or ergonomists. Their specific responsibilities vary by industry, workplace, and types of hazards affecting employees and the public.

Generally, when occupational safety and health specialists arrive at a new job site, they focus on identifying dangerous conditions and practices. They might examine machinery and equipment, like scaffolding or fume hoods, to make sure these items meet safety regulations. They may also check to make sure that protective equipment, like hard hats or safety glasses, are being used as specified by law. If a workplace has high noise levels, radiation, or dangerous chemicals, occupational safety and health specialists may prepare and calibrate scientific equipment to test the levels of these substances present in the environment. Specialists use these observations to predict hazards based on their own experience, historical data, and other information sources. In fact, these specialists may also be brought in to identify potential problems in systems, products, or processes planned for the future.

Once they develop a report of their findings, specialists set about determining a plan to eliminate potential hazards. They may consult with engineers, doctors, or other specialists to get expert advice on particular safety or health problems. Specialists may also conduct training sessions for management, supervisors, or workers to make workplaces safer and assure that companies abide by safety and health laws. Finally, they keep tabs on a plan after its implementation to see how it's working. If the plan fails to improve workplace safety, occupational health and safety specialists modify the plan accordingly.

Occupational health and safety specialists who work for government agencies are usually inspectors, checking that workplaces comply with all applicable laws and regulations. They also investigate accidents and grievances (complaints) at workplaces, conducting investigations of both the specific incident and then the entire workplace in order to determine what happened and whether it could have been prevented. Inspectors who find that health or safety regulations were not enforced can recommend legal actions.

Since specialists are constantly working to improve different job sites, the job often requires frequent travel. Occupational health and safety specialists must have a thorough understanding of all laws relating to safety standards. Explaining findings and making suggestions to managers and employees is a big part of the job, so good communication skills are mandatory. They must be detail-oriented, responsible, and good at working with all kinds of people. A strong background in math, chemistry, biology, and physics can help specialists evaluate potentially unsafe equipment and practices.

Government agencies, as well as manufacturing firms, hospitals, and consulting services, often also require occupational health and safety specialists to receive certification related to specific types of information. Certification is available through the Board of Certified Safety Professionals (***www.bcsp.org***) and the American Board of Industrial Hygiene (***www.abih.org***).

As we become more and more aware of health and safety issues in the workplace, the demand for occupational health and safety specialists continues to increase. The outlook for this career is expected to be strong in the foreseeable future.

find your paralegal future

paralegal Today's paralegals are indispensable to individual lawyers, government agencies, law firms, and corporations. Without them, there would be long waits to get legal issues taken care of, and the cost of legal support would be far higher than it already is.

Paralegals are also known as legal assistants, but they are not the same as legal secretaries. They do almost everything that lawyers do, except for those things that are specifically limited by law: accepting cases and setting fees, giving legal advice, and presenting cases in court. Paralegals are permitted to research legal precedents by going through statutes, decisions, legal articles, codes, and other documents. They can also prepare legal documents including anything from briefs and appeals for a judge to business contracts and real estate closings. In many cases, it is the paralegal who is responsible for having day to day contact with the client, conducting interviews, making sure that client and attorney each know what the other is doing, and even drafting correspondence on behalf of the attorney or client.

Paralegals routinely work on projects requiring great responsibility. Deadlines are not flexible—hearings, court proceedings, and other filings cannot be delayed because of problems in a paralegal's schedule. They may work on many projects at one time or many different aspects of one project. They may even work for several different bosses at the

Get Started Now!

- Take lots of classes in business and government to see how the legal system has influenced our country.
- Research some of the different areas of law—a good place to start is at the website of the American Bar Association (***www.abanet.org***). See which ones seem most interesting to you.
- Get up to speed with classes in typing and business writing.

Search It!

National Federation of Paralegal Associations at ***www.paralegals.org*** and National Association of Legal Assistants at ***www.nala.org***

Read It!

Legal Assistant Today at ***www.legalassistanttoday.com*** and ABA Career Page at ***www.abanet.org/legalservices/legalassistants/career.html***

Learn It!

- Associate degree in paralegal studies
- Bachelor's or master's degree in paralegal studies
- Unrelated bachelor's degree, followed by paralegal training

Earn It!

Median annual salary is $40,590 per year.
(Source: U.S. Department of Labor)

Find It!

Find current job listings at the Legal Career Center at ***http://nals.legalstaff.com***.

Hire Yourself!

See how well you do at reading and interpreting legal documents. Search the Internet for historic decisions of the Supreme Court. One good place to look is ***http://supct.law.cornell.edu/supct/index.html***. Select a case that interests you. Write a summary of the case and the decision and then write your opinion as to why this case was important enough to warrant the attention of the highest court in the land. Then search the Internet for other information about that case. See how your summary and conclusions hold up against those posted on the Internet.

same time. It's critical to be able to work well under pressure, to juggle a lot of different things at once, and to prioritize work assignments. It's also important to be able to recognize when they need help so they can seek out help in a focused way.

Like lawyers, paralegals usually specialize in a specific type of law. In the criminal and corporate litigation areas, paralegals may have to locate and interview witnesses and then write summaries of those interviews. They also research and summarize legal precedents, write briefs, and help prepare for depositions, trials, or appeals. Paralegals in the tax or probate areas need to be more familiar with tax and accounting terms and strategies. They may help prepare tax returns, draw up wills, and determine the value of a client's assets. In the corporate world, paralegals may work for a law firm specializing in corporate law or for the company itself. Either way, work may include acquisition and merger procedures, protection of intellectual property, and compliance with all relevant laws and guidelines. Those who specialize in employment law focus on labor relations, employment contracts, benefit plans, and fair employment practices. In the government sector, paralegals review proposed legislation and ensure that individuals, companies, and local governments comply with the law.

Currently, the most common way to become a paralegal is to take a two-year course at a community college. However, employers are increasingly looking for employees with a bachelor's or master's degree in paralegal studies, or a special certification program that follows a bachelor's degree. Prior work experience can be a plus.

parole and probation officer

The jobs of probation and parole officers are so similar that in some states the two jobs are actually combined into one. Both work with people who have been convicted of crimes. The probation officer's caseload is made up of people who have been convicted of crimes and who have been placed on probation, rather than being sent to prison. The parole officer's clients are offenders who have been released from prison to serve the rest of their sentence in the community.

The common purpose of both jobs is to help the people convicted of crimes become integrated back into society in a positive way. Equally, if not more important, is the goal of protecting the public and ensuring that the offender does not commit additional crimes. The officer meets with the offender, his family, and his friends to understand the challenges facing the offender and to become aware of potential problems. The officer also facilitates relationships with community service agencies that might offer additional assistance and assist with monitoring the

Get Started Now!

- Work on your word processing skills.
- It is critical to be efficient and well organized. Look for books and websites on time management. See how you can improve yours.
- Learn about the regulations regarding parole and probation in your area.
- Volunteer with people similar to those you will supervise. Consider group homes, women's shelters, prisons, support groups, and mental hospitals.

Search It!
American Probation and Parole Association at ***www.appa-net.org***

Read It!
Learn about the history of the federal parole system at ***www.usdoj.gov/uspc/history.htm***.

Learn It!
- Minimum of a bachelor's degree in social work, criminal justice, or a related field
- State or federal training program

Earn It!
Median annual salary is $38,400. (Source: U.S. Department of Labor)

Find It!
Parole and probation officers are employed by federal, state, county, and municipal governments. For federal job listings see ***www.bop.gov/recruit.html***. For state and local governments search specific state, county, or municipal websites.

Hire Yourself!

Parole and probation plans work best when the punishment fits the crime—and the criminal. The same is true when dealing with students who break school rules. Make a list of five common student infractions and come up with an appropriate punishment for each. Think of ideas that will cause students to rethink the error of their ways and avoid repeating the same mistakes. Or, when appropriate, make provisions for the student to make amends, or restitution, for property or persons damaged or wronged. Restitution and rehabilitation are important goals of the American justice system.

offender. All this information is used to develop effective rehabilitation and treatment plans.

In parole situations, much of this work begins before an offender is released into the community. The officer learns as much as possible about the offender and develops a plan with specific conditions. These conditions often spell out work requirements, travel restrictions, and infractions that can result in being sent back to prison, such as possessing firearms and illegal drug use. The parole officer is then responsible for implementing the plan and monitoring the parolee's performance on a regular basis.

Individuals on probation may be required to perform community service, make payments to victims of their crimes, or meet other requirements. In that case, the probation officer has to identify and approve appropriate situations and monitor the offender's performance at regularly scheduled intervals.

Individuals on probation, and especially individuals released on parole, may have few or no resources for living productively within the community. When this is the case, the probation or parole officer helps the offender find employment, housing, counseling, and educational resources. The officer may have to arrange for medical, mental health, or substance abuse treatment services according to individual needs and court orders.

Communication and people skills are essential in this work. The officer has to establish a relationship of trust with the offender and clearly communicate all rules of conduct, boundaries, and expectations. His or her communication style must command respect and exude authority in a way that convinces offenders to tow the line. At the same time, offenders often have problems with personal and work relationships. In those situations it can make all the difference in the world to have an officer who is approachable and able to dispense necessary advice and assistance.

If the officer suspects there has been a parole violation or that terms of the probation have been broken, he or she is required to investigate the situation. That may involve talking to the individual's friends, family, and employer. It may mean observing or searching the individual or his home, or even implementing drug tests and transporting samples to labs. If a violation has occurred, the officer must recommend remedial action or court action, which could lead to the person returning to prison.

While this type of work includes a lot of personal interaction, office work and paperwork are also large components of the job. The job includes writing evaluations and recommendations before offenders are released, keeping current and accurate files on each client's progress, and staying in contact with employers, schools, and addiction treatment centers.

Most agencies require applicants to be at least 21 years old and, for federal employment, not older than 37. People who themselves have been convicted of felonies are usually not eligible for this job. Once applicants successfully complete a training program, they usually work as trainees or in a probationary period for up to one year.

It is critical for parole and probation officers to be in good physical and emotional condition. Officers may be required to carry a firearm or other weapon for protection, and may be on call 24 hours a day to supervise and assist offenders at any time. Despite that, most probation and parole officers find great satisfaction in helping troubled people find their way back to productive and law-abiding citizenship.

Search It!
The National Association of Police Organizations at ***www.napo.org***

Read It!
Police magazine at ***www.policemag.com***

Learn It!
- Must be U.S. citizen, usually at least 20 years of age
- High school graduate
- Two- or four-year degree in law enforcement is recommended and often required

Earn It!
Median annual salary is $43,390. (Source: U.S. Department of Labor)

Find It!
Apply to local law enforcement agencies, or check websites such as ***www.lawenforcementjobs.com***.

police officer

On any given day a police officer might help track down a child separated from her mother in a crowded shopping mall or respond to the scene of a family dispute. The officer might make an arrest and stop drivers who are disobeying speed limits or stop signs. In addition, the officer might respond to a report of a burglary, a noise complaint, or a crime in progress. Many police officers are assigned to patrol a specific area, maintaining order, helping people, and enforcing the law. They may patrol on foot, by car or motorcycle, or even on horseback.

Police officers have to be alert, perceptive, and detail-oriented. They need to prevent crimes, stop crimes in progress, and keep potentially volatile situations calm and orderly. When a crime has been committed,

Get Started Now!

- Like biking? Nearly half of all local police departments and 90% of those serving at least 100,000 residents use bike patrols for police and EMS personnel. Learn about the International Police Mountain Bike Association at ***www.ipmba.org***.
- Like working with animals? Think about becoming a K9 officer. Learn more at the United States Police Canine Association at ***www.uspcak9.com***, check out the qualifications needed to be a K9 trainer at ***www.uspca3.com/trainers***, or see about becoming a foster family for a search and rescue dog from the National Disaster Search Dog Foundation at ***www.searchdogsusa.org***.
- Look for civilian jobs or volunteer opportunities with your local police organization.
- Learn some common police codes at ***www.police-central.com/police-codes.htm*** and other police terms at ***www.sacpd.org/glossary_of_terms.htm***.

Hire Yourself!

Your school has been assigned two full-time police officers. Before they assume duties, they've hired you to determine how the school can make the best use of these resources. Write brief job descriptions defining each officer's duties.

police officers pursue and arrest suspects, ultimately taking them to the local police precinct for processing. Arresting officers are required to complete detailed reports that may be used by officers who follow up on the case or by the attorneys involved in criminal trials resulting from the arrest. Police reports usually cover every aspect of the case, from details about the incident to the behavior of the suspect and the police at the time of the arrest.

Officers also help people in need. They might respond to an accident scene and provide emergency medical assistance until an ambulance arrives. Police officers also offer advice and services, such as giving a battered wife the name and location of a women's shelter. They also direct traffic in case of an emergency (like a flooded road) and talk to kids in schools about stranger safety.

An officer might work for a special unit, such as a K9 unit that uses dogs to sniff out criminals and perform rescue operations. Some officers work for the bomb squad, helping to find and safely dispose of explosives. Others are part of an elite team called Special Weapons and Tactics (SWAT). They provide extra protection, including snipers, during high-risk arrests and hostage situations.

Some police officers eventually become detectives. A detective collects facts and evidence for criminal cases. They examine crime scenes, collecting evidence like hair or clothing fibers and taking photographs of bloodstains, footprints, and anything that may seem relevant. They interview witnesses and protect the scene from being tampered with. A detective's tasks also include performing video surveillance, monitoring a criminal's Internet use, and examining police reports looking for clues.

If you're thinking of joining forces with the police force, here's what you need to know. The minimum age to be a police officer is usually 20. You need a high school diploma or a GED, at the very least. Many police forces require either an associate's degree or even a bachelor's in a field like criminal justice. After you apply, plan on taking a written test, a physical abilities test, and even a psychological exam. You also must be prepared to pass a drug test and background check. Personal characteristics such as honesty, sound judgment, integrity, and a sense of responsibility are especially important so interviews by a senior offi-

cer or by a psychiatrist or psychologist might be involved in the interview process as well.

New recruits go through three to six months of training at a Peace Officer Standards and Training Academy (POST). Training can be at either a local or regional facility and can be a day program or a residential one. The POST program includes an introduction to law enforcement, training in crowd control, and practice directing traffic, as well as instruction in self-defense, weapons, and special driving skills.

Police officers are observers, enforcers, problem solvers, and negotiators. Good officers can calm people and get information from them. They are able to work with a wide range of people and community programs and behave in ways that inspire the confidence of others.

find your future
private investigator

private investigator

The image of the private investigator who slinks around dark alleys to get the "dirt" on unfaithful spouses or to find wanted criminals is one that works well for novels, movies, and television. In real life, private investigators are just as likely to spend their time in front of a computer or in business conference rooms as they are out in the field.

Private investigators may spend their days (or nights) in an office with a telephone and a computer, in court records departments, in the homes of the rich and famous, in fancy corporate offices, or (as in the novels) in some of the least appealing bars and hangouts you can imagine.

Most private investigators use similar tools and techniques. Physical surveillance is an important part of many assignments. This involves watching a home, office, or other location, sometimes for long periods of time. It may also involve taking photographs or videos to verify the actions of an individual or to document certain activities occurring at a given location. Surveillance can be done on foot, in a vehicle, or even electronically.

Get Started Now!

- Find out the regulating agency and the licensing requirements for private investigators in your state. A good place to start is at America's Career InfoNet at ***http://tinyurl.com/3a8a4***.
- Check out the requirements for becoming a certified legal investigator through the National Association of Legal Investigators, Inc. at ***www.nalionline.org***.
- Find classes in criminal justice in your area. Look at community colleges and trade schools.

Search It!
National Association of Legal Investigators at ***www.nalionline.org***

Read It!
PI Magazine at ***www.pi.org***

Learn It!
- College degree with major in area like criminal justice or criminal science
- Prior experience in law enforcement, military, and government
- State license

Earn It!
Median annual salary is $29,300 per year.
(Source: U.S. Department of Labor)

Find It!
Investigators work for government agencies, all kinds of businesses, and insurance agencies. Many operate their own investigation companies. See ***www.pimall.com/nais/dir.menu.html*** for links to employers in your state.

Private investigators are also experts in countersurveillance, watching people and places to make sure someone else isn't spying on them too.

Good interviewing techniques are critical for private investigators. They often speak to witnesses and people who may know the subject of an investigation. Getting needed information from a source is a definite skill. Research skills are also important. Good investigators are good researchers—often finding especially creative ways to obtain information. Common types of information they seek out includes background checks, legal judgments, assets, motor vehicle information, and past addresses.

Companies and individuals hire private investigators for many different reasons, and most investigators specialize accordingly. Investigators with financial or accounting backgrounds are often called upon to look for hidden assets, especially in divorce cases or to help pay damages issued in lawsuits. They may also develop financial profiles of individuals in situations where corporate dishonesty is suspected.

Legal investigators usually work for lawyers. They may collect information about the people involved in a specific case, locate and interview witnesses, talk to police, take photographs, and testify in court. Corporations may hire investigators to look for theft or drug use within the company, "leaks" in corporate security, or other types of fraud.

The retail industry employs a great number of investigators, sometimes called store detectives or loss prevention agents. Inventory "shrinkage," employee theft, vendor fraud, and administrative errors cost the retail industry more than $31 billion in lost revenue in 2001; shoplifting cost almost $10 billion more. Given numbers like that, employing retail investigators can be a smart investment for retailers.

Private investigators offer many other services. Some provide protection for executives and celebrities. Others specialize in missing persons services. They hunt for a wide range of types of missing people:

Hire Yourself!

One of the most famous fictional private investigators of all time is the Sherlock Holmes character created by Sir Arthur Conan Doyle. Sherlock Holmes and his loyal sidekick Doctor Watson solved cases in England between 1881 and 1904. Use the Internet (or better yet, check out one of Doyle's books) to find out more about Holmes' investigative techniques. Imagine that Sherlock Holmes was a real, modern day detective. Describe how some of his techniques might or might not be useful in this day and age.

bail jumpers, witnesses, child abductors, debtors, adoption searchers, and even old lovers.

Although most private investigators are never in situations that require weapons, many find it beneficial to get appropriate weapons training and licenses as well as self-defense training. Although it is not always required, the Certified Legal Investigator designation available from the National Association of Legal Investigators provides nationally recognized credentials that can help a private investigator land a job or convince a new client to hire them.

Search It!
Association of Public-Safety Communications Officials at ***www.apco911.org*** and National Academies of Emergency Dispatch at ***www.emergencydispatch.org***

Read It!
Dispatch Monthly at ***www.911dispatch.com*** and *Journal of Emergency Dispatch* at ***www.emergencydispatch.org/JOURNAL***

Learn It!
- High school diploma
- Some states require a written or oral test

Earn It!
Median salary is $27,600 per year. (Source: U.S. Department of Labor)

Find It!
Check with your local police department, or visit ***www.911dispatch.com/job_file/JobWantAds.html***.

public safety dispatcher

A motor vehicle accident leaves a woman trapped in her mangled car. A thief with a gun holds a convenience store clerk hostage. A man awakes in his hotel room to find it full of smoke. In every one of these instances, and many more like them, police, fire, and ambulance dispatchers offer a bridge from danger to safety.

Also called public safety dispatchers, these workers answer calls from people in need and direct emergency personnel—police, firemen, and emergency medical services (EMS)—to the locations where they are needed.

When a call comes in, the dispatcher springs into action. The first task is to keep the caller calm and to determine what is actually happening. For example, when a caller says, "my house was robbed," the dispatcher tries to get more details. If it just happened, the incident will have a higher priority than if the caller came back from a two-week vacation and discovered the situation. If the caller was home at the time, or saw the suspect leaving the house, the priority will be higher still. As they talk, the dispatcher enters critical information into a computer,

Get Started Now!

- Dispatchers need to be familiar with computers to enter and retrieve information. Practice your computer and typing skills.
- Volunteer with your local fire department or EMS service.
- Check with your American Red Cross chapter about opportunities to learn CPR and first aid.

Hire Yourself!

Study the flow chart for public safety dispatching located at ***www.911dispatch.com/calltaking/calltaker.html***. Then, write a conversation that you as a dispatcher might have with a caller who called with one of the following complaints: a family comes home to find their house had been robbed (and got a quick look at the thief running away); a woman on a cellular phone calls to report that her car has skidded off the road somewhere on the highway, and now she is injured and stuck in a ditch; a young girl home alone hears gunshots down the street; a man calls to report that the linen factory he's working in is on fire.

including the nature of the emergency, the person's location, and the time of the call.

Dispatchers usually keep track of where emergency units are at all times, so they can find an appropriate unit close enough to respond to the emergency. They also relay the information to fire, police, or medical personnel.

Many areas require dispatchers to be trained in first aid and emergency procedures. A qualified dispatcher may give instructions to the caller, such as how to perform the Heimlich maneuver on a choking victim or how to stop severe bleeding. Dispatchers have even helped callers deliver babies! During this time, the dispatcher also stays in contact with the responding emergency services unit, tracking how close it is to the emergency site.

Dispatchers usually monitor police radio frequencies while they work, listening for any signs that additional help is needed. Although cities try to educate the public against this practice, many people call 911 for non-emergency calls, such as a request that an illegally parked car be towed or a call to report that their business has been vandalized with graffiti. In those cases, the dispatcher must politely refer the caller to the correct agency so that he or she can be ready to handle emergency calls.

A public safety dispatcher might work for a specific agency like the police department or for a central dispatch location that covers all of a city's or region's emergency responders. And, while most cities employ civilians as dispatchers, some still employ only police officers, firemen, and EMS personnel.

To become an emergency dispatcher, applicants must have a high school diploma and pass any required written or oral examinations. Medical tests (drug users are definitely not eligible) and psychological screening are also standard requirements. Excellent verbal skills are very important and knowledge of a second language is highly valued. People skills are also an asset; callers are often upset and it's the dispatcher's job to help calm them down and keep control of the situation.

Most training happens on the job, where new dispatchers shadow more experienced dispatchers and learn how to answer calls and use the phone system, radio equipment, and computers.

You may also participate in a ride-along with the police or EMS to observe how they handle emergencies and to learn how the dispatcher can be most helpful to them. The training period will also give you an idea of how you handle a high-stress environment. This is a job where every second counts and mistakes can be deadly!

Police, fire, and EMS dispatchers provide a valuable service to the community. The work can be frantic and upsetting. But it can also be exciting as well as fulfilling, as dispatchers can take pride in knowing that they help save lives.

find your future public safety diver

public safety diver

You've probably heard that water covers two-thirds of the earth's surface. That's a big area. It's also an area where accidents occur and crimes are committed. Public safety divers, also called dive rescue specialists, are called to help in situations where humans and water don't mix. For instance, they come to the rescue when boating mishaps leave people stranded in the water or in cases where someone is in danger of drowning. Much like firefighters and other rescue workers, public safety divers work under circumstances where people's lives often depend on them doing their job well.

Public safety dive teams often work in less-than-favorable conditions. They must often go down to great depths in ice-cold water, with low—if any—visibility. It is therefore imperative that rescue divers learn a variety of skills, such as observation, navigation, and diving techniques.

Skills like this are only gained in one way—through lots of practice.

When a water crisis occurs, public safety divers receive written or verbal instructions before beginning the dive. They are assigned carefully outlined areas to search—usually involving areas between 270 and 360 square feet at a time. They work in teams, are attached to a tether, and communicate with surface support personnel such as boat operators and paramedics via telephones and signal lines. Rescue divers use scuba

Get Started Now!

- Classes in math, science, and criminology (if it is offered) will help.
- Take scuba lessons or try out for the school swim team. If those options aren't available to you, then anything you can do to get in shape is a good start!
- Dive into the dictionary of diving terms at ***www.SanDiegoDiving.com/resources/dictionary/***.

Search It!

The International Association of Public Safety Diving at ***www.publicsafetydiver.com*** and National Academy of Police Diving (NAPD) at ***www.policediver.com***

Read It!

Dive rescue news at ***www.iadrs.org***

Learn It!

- 100+ hours of dive rescue and recovery training
- Law enforcement certification for police divers

Earn It!

Median annual salary is $34,710. (Source: U.S. Department of Labor)

Find It!

Apply through your local law enforcement agency for a job as a police diver. Search for a local dive rescue team, like this one for Spokane, Washington: ***www.spokanewaterrescue.org***.

Hire Yourself!

You have been hired by a local police station to set up a public safety dive squad. As squad leader, the first thing you have to do is equip the team with the necessary equipment. Go on-line to resources like ***www.Scuba.com*** and download pictures of the types of equipment each diver will need to do his or her job safely and effectively. Use those pictures to create a poster illustrating each piece of equipment and describing its function.

gear and diving suits to do their work. Both the gear and the suit allow them to withstand the elements and dive deeper and to work underwater for longer periods of time.

Public safety divers can also work for law enforcement agencies. Police divers, as they are called when they work in this capacity, have slightly different responsibilities. They often work under slightly less pressure, since their dives are usually an effort to retrieve bodies or evidence, rather than to rescue a live human being. These divers look for lost or stolen property, sunken ships and vehicles, explosives, evidence of a crime committed, and countless other things. Police divers need to know how to handle evidence properly and how to operate devices such as underwater cameras.

Commercial divers perform these types of tasks in addition to assisting in underwater demolition and construction. These types of jobs often require other types of skills in addition to diving. For instance, commercial divers may be required to weld underwater structures together or repair submerged equipment. Divers are often required to work in different types of water too—different jobs call for work in lakes, oceans, rivers, quarries, reservoirs, and even sewers.

Many hours of training are necessary to become a public safety diver. Dive rescue courses offer instruction in scene evaluation, incident debriefing, diving equipment, media relations, search pattern fundamentals, and accident scene documentation. Other courses include those that instruct a diver in underwater technology, hazardous dive conditions, and salvage and recovery. Most courses last three to three and a half days, and involve both classroom training as well as actual dives.

Of course, there's more to this job than diving. Divers must write follow-up reports after dives and are sometimes asked to offer testimony in court. Successful divers are strong both physically and mentally and are committed to doing whatever it takes to get the job done.

recreational services safety specialist

Accidents happen. It's just a simple fact of life. When accidents happen in parks, at beaches, or on ski slopes, it is often recreational services safety specialists who come to the rescue. If the accident happens at a beach, a public pool, or resort a lifeguard is the most likely source of help. If things go awry on a ski slope, much needed assistance comes from the ski patrol.

Since skiing and swimming are both outdoor activities, weather can have a major impact on the safety of participants. Lifeguards and ski patrollers should have a good knowledge of weather patterns and warning signs and must be able to convey that knowledge to others when conditions become dangerous. Ski patrollers must stay aware of avalanches, storms, and frostbite, while lifeguards must gain a certain expertise in

Get Started Now!

- Get certified in first aid and CPR though your local Red Cross or other organization.
- Practice your skills in swimming or skiing. Many areas have a pretest to evaluate your skills before you can even qualify to take the training or final test.
- Learn about weather trends and potential dangers in the area in which you want to work.
- Learn some of the basics of ski rescue and avalanche safety at ***www.patrol.org/instructor***.

Search It!

National Ski Patrol at ***www.nsp.org*** and United States Lifesaving Association at ***www.usla.org***

Read It!

Ski Patrol magazine at ***www.nsp.org/nsp2002/spm*** and *A Lifesaving Story* at ***www.usla.org/LGtoLG/story.asp***

Learn It!

- High school diploma or GED
- CPR certification, possibly EMT certification
- On-the-job training

Earn It!

Salaries for lifeguards and ski patrollers depend on the area and on the length of the season.

Find It!

Find opportunities for all kinds of recreational service safety specialists at the National Park Service website at ***www.nps.gov/personnel/other.htm***.

currents, hurricanes, and other water perils (such as sharks). They also prevent problems by enforcing all rules in the recreational area.

Ski patrollers are often responsible for inspecting equipment such as rope tows, T-bars, J-bars, and chairlifts to make sure that they are safe and not showing signs of wear or damage. They may also provide instruction in the safe use of that equipment. Some ski patrollers monitor snow for signs of avalanches and may even try to prevent avalanches by starting them when no skiers are on the slopes. They also have to be prepared to handle incidents with many injuries at once.

Becoming a member of the Professional Ski Patrol Association requires passing a variety of skill tests including skiing abilities and rescue procedures. It also requires proven proficiency in first aid. A ski patroller's proficiency is tested in two ways. One involves a written exam on outdoor emergency care. It also involves a practical exam that features actual simulations of different types of emergency situations. Finally, a face-to-face encounter with an experienced interviewer is used to evaluate potential ski patrollers' knowledge of ski patrol operations.

Lifeguards watch swimmers to make sure they remain in approved areas and to see if they need help. Those working at beaches may use special four-wheel drive vehicles to respond to major emergencies, such as beached boats or cliff accidents. Lifeguards working at pools may also be responsible for testing the water and maintaining desired pH values and chlorine content.

Lifeguards must pass vigorous tests. Most employers use those who meet standards established by the American Red Cross and require that lifeguards be certified in CPR (cardiopulmonary resuscitation) and first aid.

Both types of recreational services safety specialists are also challenged by growing numbers of active senior citizens. Many older

Hire Yourself!

You have just been hired as director of safety for a major resort. One of your first jobs is to create a program for children that will reinforce all safety measures that they should implement. You may choose whether you want to be at a ski resort or a beach resort. Your program should be interesting to children who are three to nine years old. It should instruct them about what to do in different emergencies. Create a poster or brief PowerPoint presentation that you could use to describe your program to young participants.

Americans' active lifestyles include time on the slopes and in the waters. While older people may (or may not) be more cautious about the risks they take, they are also more prone to heart attacks and strokes, and their bones are more likely to break if they fall.

No matter the age of the injured person or the type of the terrain, recreational service safety specialists must be able to respond quickly, with able body and focused mind to bring the person to safety, perform necessary and sometimes life-saving emergency procedures, and provide transportation to appropriate medical treatment facilities.

Search It!
Aerial Firefighting Industry Association at ***www.afia.com*** and National Interagency Fire Center (NIFC) at ***www.nifc.gov***

Read It!
Fire Engineering magazine at ***http://fe.pennnet.com*** and Fire and Aviation Management at ***www.fs.fed.us/fire***

Learn It!
- High school diploma or GED
- Pass a rigorous physical fitness test
- Complete specialized firefighting training

Earn It!
Median annual salary is $37,530 per year.
(Source: U.S. Department of Labor)

Find It!
Find job listings at the USDA Forest Service website at ***www.fs.fed.us/fsjobs***.

wildland firefighter

In nature, forest fires are a natural and inevitable occurrence. These fires help clear out old growth and prepare forests for renewal. In that sense, forest fires are a good thing.

However, in cases when forest fires are caused by arson or carelessness or when fires rage out of control, wildland fires can be very bad. Every year, forests burn down, homes are threatened or destroyed, and lives are lost. In 2002 alone, there were more than 88,000 forest fires, and almost 7 million acres of land were destroyed.

States in high-risk areas like California and Colorado and government agencies such as the Bureau of Land Management, National Park Service, Forest Service, Bureau of Indian Affairs, and the U.S. Fish and Wildlife Service employ wildland firefighters to control and extinguish fires in forests and other public lands. These firefighters work in planes, in helicopters, and on the ground.

Fighting wildland fires requires a huge technical and well-coordinated effort. The Fire and Aviation division of the U.S. Forest Service

Get Started Now!

- Check out the different agencies involved in wildland fire management. Links to all of them can be found on the National Interagency Fire Center website at ***www.nifc.gov***.
- Learn more about firefighting aircraft from the Aerial Firefighting Industry Association at ***www.afia.com***.
- Learn the lingo! Study the NIFC's glossary of wildland fire terms at ***www.nifc.gov/fireinfo/glossary.html***.
- Follow a U.S. Forest Service Hotshot Crew as they fight forest fires at ***www.sover.net/~kenandeb/fire/hotshot.html***.

Hire Yourself!

Use resources you find at the USDA Forest Service website at ***www.fs.fed.us*** and by using an Internet search engine to find information about "national forest fires" to create either a state or national map showing the locations of at least six forest fire "hot spots." Hot spots may include national parks and other areas susceptible to wildland fires.

works to advance these technologies and to support federal, state, and international partners.

The key jobs in fighting wildland fires include the following:

- Smokejumpers are the firefighters who parachute from planes to fight the fire. Smokejumpers generally make the first attacks on fires in remote or inaccessible areas. It takes a lot of experience, working as many as four to five seasons, to even be considered to be a smokejumper.
- Engine crews do most of the essential work of the team. As you can imagine, wildland fire engines are very different from those used to fight municipal fires. They are usually heavy-duty off road vehicles. Each carries a crew of three to five firefighters, up to 800 gallons of water, and foam to use on wildland fuels or to protect the exterior walls of a building.
- Hand crews are teams of about 20 firefighters each. Although the members of the hand crews have been trained to fight fire, their everyday jobs are usually in some other area of forest management.
- The hotshot fire crews usually get the toughest assignments in major forest fires. These highly trained and experienced crews use specialized hand tools and are usually on duty for four months at a time.

Wildland firefighters on the ground are supported by a battery of aircraft. Helicopters drop water, foam, or other retardants to cool hot spots and prevent a fire from spreading. Helicopters also carry helitack crews, specialists who load and unload "slings" of equipment and supplies by rappelling from a hovering helicopter where there is no place for the aircraft to land. Airtankers, with capacities of up to 3,000 gallons of water or fire retardant, lead planes, and infrared planes are also used in the fight.

Fighting a wildland fire involves much more than knowing how to face the flames. Firefighters have to be proficient with hand tools like axes, shovels, and chainsaws so that they can cut down trees, clear brush, and dig trenches, creating boundaries so there is no more fuel for the fire to spread further. They must cultivate excellent orienteering skills, so they can quickly find supplies and equipment that have been dropped from planes. They need to be able to maintain contact with each other and with dispatchers at all times—teamwork is an essential aspect of the job. After all or part of a fire is put out, firefighters remain to patrol the burned areas, looking for hot spots that might rekindle the fire.

When they are not actively involved in a fire, wildland firefighters continue to work on physical strength and endurance. They attend classes to learn about new equipment and techniques, maintain all equipment, and participate in fire education, prevention, and inspection programs.

Woodland firefighters must be physically fit, self-confident, and able to remain calm in emergencies. They should enjoy working as part of a team and be able to communicate clearly and concisely. Most agencies want their woodland firefighters to be between 18 and 35 years of age.

Search It!
Federal Wildlife Officers Association at ***www.fwoa.org*** and North American Wildlife Enforcement Officers Association at ***www.naweoa.org***

Read It!
National Wildlife magazine at ***www.nwf.org/nationalwildlife/***

Learn It!
- Minimum of high school diploma
- Law enforcement experience or college degree in related field

Earn It!
Median annual salary is $41,010. (Source: U.S. Department of Labor)

Find It!
Wildlife conservation officers work for individual states or federal government. Find job listings for most states at ***www.fwoa.org/jobs.html***.

find your future wildlife conservation officer

wildlife conservation officer

Wildlife conservation officers used to be known as fish and game wardens. Most people thought of them as the enforcers of hunting and fishing laws—making sure that everyone had the correct license, was hunting or fishing only during the designated season, and didn't take more than the maximum allotment of fish or animals. In order to recognize all of the other equally important aspects of the job, most states now use different titles for these positions. The most common titles are wildlife conservation officer, environmental warden, and conservation officer. A simple description of the job is that wildlife conservation officers are the police of the woods and waters.

Due to differences in both the terrain and the types of fish and wildlife that reside in various parts of the country, the responsibilities of these positions vary greatly among the states. The essence of the job is still the enforcement of state fish and game laws. In states like Florida, there is more emphasis on fish, while other states emphasize bears, deer, clams, or lobster.

In order to enforce these laws, wildlife conservation officers patrol assigned areas, looking for violators. Depending on the terrain, patrolling may be conducted by car, boat, airplane, horse, or on foot. In some states, officers may use decoy animals to flush out hunters who

Get Started Now!

- Get comfortable in front of a group. Give talks wherever you can—to scout groups, classes, clubs.
- Take classes in biology and environmental sciences.
- Look up the appropriate agency in your state to learn about the laws pertaining to hunting, fishing, and wildlife.

Hire Yourself!

Go on-line to ***www.fwoa.org/links.html*** at the Federal Wildlife Officers Association website. Click on the link to your state and use the resources you find to create a poster describing your state's wildlife priorities.

are hunting in the wrong season, not wearing the required orange safety gear, or shooting in an unacceptable location. When officers find people who are not respecting the law, they can write tickets or make arrests. They can also confiscate any equipment used in the violation and arrange for disposition of fish and game that were illegally taken.

Another major focus of the job is collecting data on the populations of various wildlife and monitoring the habitats and food supplies necessary to sustain those animal populations.

Wildlife conservation officers also investigate damage that wildlife can cause to crops or property. They come up against a wide variety of events: wolves attacking flocks of sheep, coyotes attacking pets, beavers clogging water pipes, and other kinds of animal damage to crops. In those situations, the officer becomes a detective, trying to determine from tracks and droppings what kind of animal was to blame, how future damage can be avoided, and how much the property owner should be reimbursed.

Officers investigate all accidents involving animals, hunters, and other people. Their job also has an important educational component. They speak at schools and to other groups to emphasize the importance of wildlife conservation. In many states they teach required hunter-trapper education in classes that may feature everything from firearm safety to training in ethical behavior and showing respect for others and the resources.

The role of the wildlife conservation officer now often includes the enforcement of laws pertaining to boating, motor vehicles, criminal acts, and public safety. Some officers assist and serve as backup for police in cases involving drugs, assaults, domestic disputes, and other situations.

Do you think you'd like to become a wildlife conservation officer? You'll have to meet the minimum age requirement (between 19 and 21, depending on the state). You'll need to be in really good physical condition and pass a fitness test. Some states have minimum requirements for vision as well. You'll also have to take a civil service test or other test that measures reading comprehension, math, and language skills.You usually have to be a citizen of the United States. Experience in the military, law enforcement, or college degrees are all helpful in this field. Once you are accepted as a trainee, you enter a training program in your state. Depending on the state, training can last from six to 18 months.

Big Question #5: do you have the right skills?

Career exploration is, in one sense, career matchmaking. The goal is to match your basic traits, interests and strengths, work values, and work personality with viable career options.

But the "stuff" you bring to a job is only half of the story.

Choosing an ideal job and landing your dream job is a two-way street. Potential employers look for candidates with specific types of skills and backgrounds. This is especially true in our technology-infused, global economy.

In order to find the perfect fit, you need to be fully aware of not only what you've got, but also what prospective employers need.

The following activity is designed to help you accomplish just that. This time we'll use the "wannabe" approach —working with careers you think you want to consider. This same matchmaking process will come in handy when it comes time for the real thing too.

Unfortunately, this isn't one of those "please turn to the end of the chapter and you'll find all the answers" types of activities. This one requires the best critical thinking, problem-solving, and decision-making skills you can muster.

Here's how it works:

Step 1: First, make a chart like the one on page 130.

Step 2: Next, pick a career profile that interests you and use the following resources to compile a list of the traits and skills needed to be successful. Include:

- Information featured in the career profile in this book;
- Information you discover when you look through websites of any of the professional associations or other resources listed with each career profile;
- Information from the career profiles and skills lists found on-line at America's Career InfoNet at ***www.acinet.org***.

Briefly list the traits or skills you find on separate lines in the first column of your chart.

Step 3: Evaluate yourself as honestly as possible. If, after careful consideration, you conclude that you already possess one of the traits or skills included on your list, place an *X* in the column marked "Got It!" If you conclude that the skill or trait is one you've yet to acquire, follow these directions to complete the column marked "Get It!":

- If you believe that gaining proficiency in a skill is just a matter of time and experience and you're willing to do whatever it takes to acquire that skill, place a *Y* (for yes) in the corresponding space.
- Or, if you are quite certain that a particular skill is one that you don't possess now, and either can't or won't do what it takes to acquire it, mark the corresponding space with an *N* (for no). For example, you want to be a brain surgeon. It's important, prestigious work and the pay is good. But, truth be told, you'd rather have brain surgery yourself than sit through eight more years of really intense science and math. This rather significant factor may or may not affect your ultimate career choice. But it's better to think it through now rather than six years into med school.

Step 4: Place your completed chart in your Big Question AnswerBook.

When you work through this process carefully, you should get some eye-opening insights into the kinds of careers that are right for you. Half reality check and half wake-up call, this activity lets you see how you measure up against important workforce competencies.

Big Activity #5: **do you have the right skills?**

skill or trait required	got it!	get it!

GOT IT!

GET IT!

more career ideas in law and public safety

Careers featured in the previous section represent mainstream, highly viable occupations where someone with the right set of skills and training stands more than half a chance of finding gainful employment. However, these ideas are just the beginning. There are lots of ways to make a living in any industry—and this one is no exception.

Following is a list of career ideas related in one way or another to law and public safety. This list is included here for two reasons. First, to illustrate some unique ways to blend your interests with opportunities. Second, to keep you thinking beyond the obvious.

As you peruse the list you are sure to encounter some occupations you've never heard of before. Good. We hope you get curious enough to look them up. Others may trigger one of those "aha" moments where everything clicks and you know you're onto something good. Either way we hope it helps point the way toward some rewarding opportunities in law and public safety.

Alcohol, Tobacco, Firearms and Explosives (ATF) Officer

Animal Control Officer

Armored Car Guards

Arson Investigator

Attorney

Campus Security Guard

Canine Handler

Case Worker

Certified Security Officer

Chemical Dependency Counselor

Child Protection Officer

Child Support Enforcement Officer

Computer Forensics Examiner

Computer Security Engineer

Computer Security Technician

Control Center Operator

Correctional Officer

Correctional Treatment Specialist

Corrections Case Manager

Corrections Educator

Court Interpreter

Criminal Investigator

Criminal Justice
Social Worker

Deputy Sheriff

Detective

Detention Officer

Drug Enforcement
Adminstration (DEA) Officer

Emergency Management and
Response Coordinator

Environmental Compliance
Officer

Evidence Technician

Executive Protection Officer

Explosives Technician

Facility Security Manager

Federal Agent

Federal Marshal

Forensic Accountant

Forensic Dentist

Forensic Engineer

Forensic Psychologist

Forensic Technician

Forest Firefighter

Highway Patrol Officer

Industrial Espionage
Security Officer

Investigative Assistant

Jail Administrator

Law Clerk

Legislator

Life Guard

Loss Control Supervisor

Loss Prevention Manager

Magistrate

Military Serviceperson

National Guard Officer

National Guard Troop

Negotiator

911 Operator

Park Ranger

Polygraph Examiner

Prison Guard

Probation Officer

Protection Manager

Rescue Worker

Search and Rescue Worker

Security Director

Security Guard

Security Systems Designer

Security Systems Technician

Security Trainer

Sheriff

Ski Patrol

Social Worker

State Trooper

Store Detective

Substance Abuse Counselor

Transportation Security
Supervisor

Treasury Agent

United States Marshal

Utilities Security Specialist

Warden

Big Question #6: are you on the right path?

You've covered a lot of ground so far. You've had a chance to discover more about your own potential and expectations. You've taken some time to explore the realities of a wide variety of career opportunities within this industry.

Now is a good time to sort through all the details and figure out what all this means to you. This process involves equal measures of input from your head and your heart. Be honest, think big, and, most of all, stay true to you.

You may be considering an occupation that requires years of advanced schooling which, from your point of view, seems an insurmountable hurdle. What do you do? Give up before you even get started? We hope not. We'd suggest that you try some creative thinking.

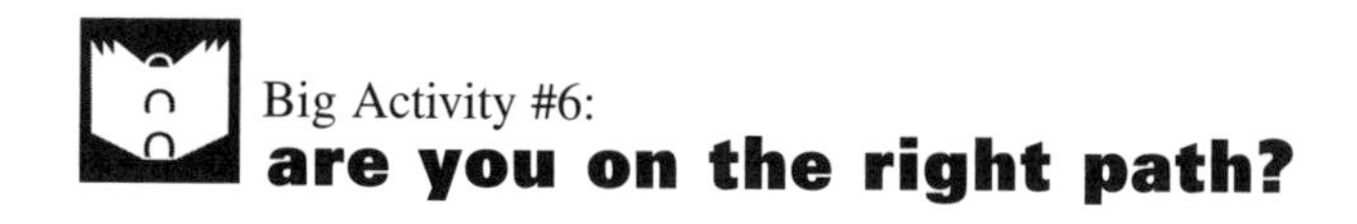

Big Activity #6:

are you on the right path?

Start by asking yourself if you want to pursue this particular career so badly that you're willing to do whatever it takes to make it. Then stretch your thinking a little to consider alternative routes, nontraditional career paths, and other equally meaningful occupations.

Following are some prompts to help you sort through your ideas. Simply jot down each prompt on a separate sheet of notebook paper and leave plenty of space for your responses.

Big Activity #6: **are you on the right path?**

ARE YOU ON THE RIGHT PATH?

One thing I know for sure about my future occupation is

I'd prefer to pursue a career that offers

I'd prefer to pursue a career that requires

A career option I'm now considering is

What appeals to me most about this career is

What concerns me most about this career is

Things that I still need to learn about this career include

Big Activity #6: **are you on the right path?**

Another career option I'm considering is

What appeals to me most about this career is

What concerns me most about this career is

Things that I still need to learn about this career include

Of these two career options I've named, the one that best fits most of my interests, skills, values, and work personality is because

At this point in the process, I am

❑ Pretty sure I'm on the right track

❑ Not quite sure yet but still interested in exploring some more

❑ Completely clueless about what I want to do

ARE YOU ON THE RIGHT PATH?

experiment with success

Right about now you may find it encouraging to learn that the average person changes careers five to seven times in his or her life. Plus, most college students change majors several times. Even people who are totally set on what they want to do often end up being happier doing something just a little bit different from what they first imagined.

So, whether you think you've found the ultimate answer to career happiness or you're just as confused as ever, you're in good company. The best advice for navigating these important life choices is this: Always keep the door open to new ideas.

As smart and dedicated as you may be, you just can't predict the future. Some of the most successful professionals in any imaginable field could never ever have predicted what—and how—they would be doing what they actually do today. Why? Because when they were in high school those jobs didn't even exist. It was not too long ago that there were no such things as personal computers, Internet research, digital cameras, mass e-mails, cell phones, or any of the other newfangled tools that are so critical to so many jobs today.

Keeping the door open means being open to recognizing changes in yourself as you mature and being open to changes in the way the world works. It also involves a certain willingness to learn new things and tackle new challenges.

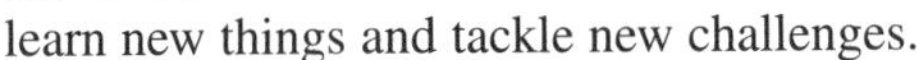

It's easy to see how being open to change can sometimes allow you to go further in your chosen career than you ever dreamed. For instance, in almost any profession you can imagine, technology has fueled unprecedented opportunities. Those people and companies who have embraced this "new way of working" have often surpassed their original expectations of success. Just ask Bill Gates. He's now one of the world's wealthiest men thanks to a company called Microsoft that he cofounded while still a student at Harvard University.

It's a little harder to see, but being open to change can also mean that you may have to let go of your first dream and find a more appropriate one. Maybe your dream is to become a professional athlete. At this point in your life you may think that there's nothing in the world that would possibly make you happier. Maybe you're right and maybe you have the talent and persistence (and the lucky breaks) to take you all the way.

But maybe you don't. Perhaps if you opened yourself to new ideas you'd discover that the best career involves blending your interest in sports with your talent in writing to become a sports journalist or sports information director. Maybe your love of a particular sport and your interest in working with children might best be served in a coaching career. Who knows what you might achieve when you open yourself to all the possibilities?

So, whether you've settled on a career direction or you are still not sure where you want to go, there are several "next steps" to consider. In this section, you'll find three more Big Questions to help keep your career planning moving forward. These Big Questions are:

? Big Question #7: **who knows what you need to know?**

? Big Question #8: **how can you find out what a career is really like?**

? Big Question #9: **how do you know when you've made the right choice?**

Big Question #7: who knows what you need to know?

When it comes to the nitty-gritty details about what a particular job is really like, who knows what you need to know? Someone with a job like the one you want, of course. They'll have the inside scoop—important information you may never find in books or websites. So make talking to as many people as you can part of your career planning process.

Learn from them how they turned their own challenges into opportunities, how they got started, and how they made it to where they are now. Ask the questions that aren't covered in "official" resources, such as what it is really like to do their job, how they manage to do a good job and have a great life, how they learned what they needed to learn to do their job well, and the best companies or situations to start in.

A good place to start with these career chats or "informational interviews" is with people you know—or more likely, people you know who know people with jobs you find interesting. People you already know include your parents (of course), relatives, neighbors, friends' parents, people who belong to your place of worship or club, and so on.

All it takes to get the process going is gathering up all your nerve and asking these people for help. You'll find that nine and a half times out of 10, the people you encounter will be delighted to help, either by providing information about their careers or by introducing you to people they know who can help.

hints and tips for a successful interview

• TIP #1

Think about your goals for the interview, and write them down.

Be clear about what you want to know after the interview that you didn't know before it.

Remember that the questions for all personal interviews are not the same. You would probably use different questions to write a biography of the person, to evaluate him or her for a job, to do a history of the industry, or to learn about careers that might interest you.

Writing down your objectives will help you stay focused.

• TIP #2

Pay attention to how you phrase your questions.

Some questions that we ask people are "closed" questions; we are looking for a clear answer, not an elaboration. "What time does the movie start?" is a good example of a closed question.

Sometimes, when we ask a closed question, we shortchange ourselves. Think about the difference between "What times are the showings tonight?" and "Is there a 9 P.M. showing?" By asking the second question, you may not find out if there is an 8:45 or 9:30 show.

That can be frustrating. It usually seems so obvious when we ask a question that we expect a full answer. It's important to remember, though, that the person hearing the question doesn't always have the same priorities or know why the question is being asked.

The best example of this? Think of the toddler who answers the phone. When the caller asks, "Is your mom home?" the toddler says, "Yes" and promptly hangs up. Did the child answer the question? As far as he's concerned, he did a great job!

Another problem with closed questions is that they sometimes require so many follow-up questions that the person being interviewed feels like a suspect in an interrogation room.

A series of closed questions may go this way:

> ***Q: What is your job title?***
> A: Assistant Producer
> ***Q: How long have you had that title?***
> A: About two years.

Q: What was your title before that?
Q: How long did you have that title?
Q: What is the difference between the two jobs?
Q: What did you do before that?
Q: Where did you learn to do this job?
Q: How did you advance from one job to the next?

An alternative, "open" question invites conversation. An open-question interview might begin this way:

I understand you are an Assistant Producer. I'm really interested in what that job is all about and how you got to be at the level you are today.

Open questions often begin with words like:

Tell me about . . .
How do you feel about . . .
What was it like . . .

• TIP #3

Make the person feel comfortable answering truthfully. In general, people don't want to say things that they think will make them look bad. How to get at the truth? Be empathic, and make their answers seem "normal."

Ask a performer or artist how he or she feels about getting a bad review from the critics, and you are unlikely to hear, "It really hurts. Sometimes I just want to cry and get out of the business." Or "Critics are so stupid. They never understand what I am trying to do."

Try this approach instead: "So many people in your industry find it hard to deal with the hurt of a bad critical review. How do you handle it when that happens?"

ask the experts

You can learn a lot by interviewing people who are already successful in the types of careers you're interested in. In fact, we followed our own advice and interviewed several people who have been successful in the fields of law and public safety to share with you here.

Before you get started on your own interview, take a few minutes to look through the results of some of ours. To make it easier for you to compare the responses of all the people we interviewed, we have presented our interviews as a panel discussion that reveals important success lessons these people have learned along the way. Each panelist is introduced on the next page.

Our interviewees gave us great information about things like what their jobs are really like, how they got to where they are, and even provided a bit of sage advice for people like you who are just getting started.

So Glad You Asked

In addition to the questions we asked in the interviews in this book, you might want to add some of these questions to your own interviews:

- How did your childhood interests relate to your choice of career path?
- How did you first learn about the job you have today?
- In what ways is your job different from how you expected it to be?
- Tell me about the parts of your job that you really like.
- If you could get someone to take over part of your job for you, what aspect would you most like to give up?
- If anything were possible, how would you change your job description?
- What kinds of people do you usually meet in your work?
- Walk me through the whole process of getting your type of product made and distributed. Tell me about all the people who are involved.
- Tell me about the changes you have seen in your industry over the years. What do you see as the future of the industry?
- Are there things you would do differently in your career if you could do it all over?

real people with real jobs in law and public safety

Following are introductions to our panel of experts. Get acquainted with their backgrounds and then use their job titles to track their stories throughout the seven success lessons.

- **Terri Arnold** is a supervisory **Customs and Border Protection Officer** who works for the U.S. Department of Homeland Security in Portal, North Dakota.
- **Robert Glaser** is a police sergeant and **Canine Handler** who works in the Baton Rouge Police Department in Baton Rouge, Louisiana.
- **Carrie Stuart Parks** is a **Forensic Artist** who lives and works in Cataldo, Idaho.
- **Captain Wayne Polette** is a firefighter, paramedic, and rescue diver with the St. Louis County Metro West Fire Protection District in Missouri.
- **Lieutenant Laura Rodriguez** works with the Santa Clara County Department of Correction in California.
- **Daniel B. Vasquez** is a self-employed **Corrections and Investigative Consultant** based in Antioch, California.

Terri Arnold

Robert Glaser

Carrie Stuart Parks

Captain Wayne Polette

Success Lesson #1:

Work is a good thing when you find the right career.

- **Tell us what it's like to work in your current career.**

Customs and Border Protection Officer: My job involves enforcing laws from many different government agencies. These agencies, as well as Customs, have laws concerning what can and can't be brought into this country and laws that regulate how and under what circumstances things can be brought in. There are also a lot of laws regulating people coming into our country, and we enforce these, too.

Everyone knows that we try to keep illegal drugs from coming into the country, but at the borders, we deal with everything from missing children to preventing someone from infringing on a copyright or trademark. Our focus since the September 11th attacks has shifted more towards trying to detect people coming in that could be terrorists, or finding items that could be brought into the country and used by terrorists. We also look for people smuggling large amounts of money, because this could lead to a drug smuggling or terrorist operation.

We have very unique authority at the border. When the police or FBI or anyone else wants to search anyone or their house or belongings, they have to get a search warrant issued by a judge. When someone comes to the border, we can search their belongings, vehicles, everything. We can also do a search of the person if we suspect they are hiding something in their clothing. Our motto is that "we are America's front line," and in many ways, this is very true. We are the last line of defense before someone or something enters the country with the intention of harming our country.

Canine Handler: I have the best job in the world. I get paid to do the things I loved to do as a kid—be the police and play with a dog. And I get paid to do both—did I mention that?

Forensic Artist: Forensic art is drawing crime scenes, composites, facial reconstructions, courtroom sketches, and a host of other skills. The word forensic comes from the Roman Forum, where issues of law and philosophy were discussed and debated. Today we use the term to describe a debate team, as in a high school forensic team, or anything pertaining to law enforcement or legal proceedings.

Lieutenant: I started working as a correctional officer in 1990 and was promoted to sergeant in 1994. I was recently promoted from sergeant to lieutenant. It is a position which carries more responsibility and exciting new challenges.

Corrections and Investigative Consultant: I've enjoyed a long, successful career doing many different kinds of jobs

Everybody has to start somewhere!

Following is a list of first jobs once held by our esteemed panel of experts.

Fast food clerk

Nurse's aid

Correctional officer

Survey crew chainman (involved cutting brush with a cane knife)

in corrections. Now, I'm a semi-retired corrections and investigative consultant which means that I share the knowledge I have gained over the years with other people. I loved working in corrections; it was exciting and different every day.

Captain: My job is that of public service. As a firefighter, paramedic, and rescue diver, I am at the beck and call of the public 24 hours a day while on duty. I work 24-hour shifts where I check and clean equipment, train and study, relax and workout, and most important, respond to calls. At times my work can be very dangerous as I am expected to put my life on the line to save others. Other times it is quite fun and exciting. As a rescue diver, I can also be called at home to search for anything underwater. I respond to swift water emergencies during floods and look for lost family members that may have drowned.

Success Lesson #2: Career goals change and so do you.

- **When you were in high school, what career did you hope to pursue?**

Customs and Border Protection Officer: I hoped to pursue a career in nursing.

Canine Handler: Actually, I wanted to be a professional baseball player. My dad and brother both played professionally.

Forensic Artist: No one had ever heard of a forensic artist when I was in high school, although the FBI and the city of New York employed them. I wanted to be a teacher, and I am because I teach forensic art.

Lieutenant: I always wanted to be a police officer.

Corrections and Investigative Consultant: I was interested in working for some type of industry.

Captain: I always wanted to be a firefighter, professional scuba diver, or pilot. Today I am proud to say that I am all three.

- **What was it that made you change directions?**

Customs and Border Protection Officer: After I married, we moved to a town on the Canadian border where the best jobs were with the federal government. I started as a part-time inspector, and intended to finish nursing school some time later, but ended up staying as a customs officer.

Canine Handler: I got a scholarship to play baseball at the college level. However, my playing days ended there. After baseball fell through, I went with my second career choice of law enforcement.

Lieutenant: I got sidetracked for a little while and ended up working at a bank and going to school part time. While there I eventually climbed the ladder of success to become branch manager. But at the age of 29, I decided it was time to do what I had always wanted to do. I applied with the Department of Correction in 1989 and the rest is history.

Corrections and Investigative Consultant: Ironically enough, I got into a bit of trouble with the law when I was younger. So it was my probation officer who told me about an opportunity in corrections when I went to say hello to him after being discharged from the U.S. Army.

Captain: I pursued my dreams, went to school and never gave up. After getting into the fire service I continued to better myself and today hold the rank of Captain. As a diver I wanted to be the best, and today I am a dive instructor. I am also currently studying to become a flight instructor.

Success Lesson #3: One thing leads to another along any career path.

- **How did you end up doing what you're doing now?**

Canine Handler: I applied for the Baton Rouge Police Department and went through the lengthy process to get hired. After several years, I felt the Department wasn't going to hire me (even though I scored 100% twice on their standard testing), so I put in applications in Dallas, Texas and with the East Baton Rouge Sheriff Office (EBRSO). I eventually went to work for EBRSO and was assigned to the prison.

After a year of working at the prison, I received a call from the Baton Rouge Police Department and was informed I had been accepted to begin the Academy. While in the Academy I was exposed to the different divisions within the police department. Canine struck my interest at this time but I was advised it would be three years before I could apply for this division. After graduating from the basic academy (second in my class) I was assigned the uniform patrol division. After a year in U.P. I was transferred to the detective division where I worked armed robberies and burglaries. After two years, I applied and was accepted in the canine division. I went through basic training (three months) with my K9 Partner (the first of four partners). That was 17 years ago. Presently I am a shift supervisor/canine handler/canine trainer for the division. Also, I am an entry team member on the SRT (special response team).

Forensic Artist: My dad was the director of the North Idaho Regional Crime lab. He would bring home cases and ask me to prepare them for court. He later sent me to the FBI Academy to learn more about the field.

Lieutenant: I started out as a custody support assistant, went to the Correctional Officer Academy in April 1990, and began working as an officer in July 1990. I was promoted to sergeant in July 1994. I was recently promoted to lieutenant.

Success Lesson #4: There's more than one way to get an education.

- **Where did you learn the skills of your field, both formally (school) and informally (experience)?**

Customs and Border Protection Officer: Learning how to work hard has been important. And so has learning how to ask questions. When I don't understand something I keep asking questions until I understand the whole picture and things make sense. Sometimes this annoys people but this trait has helped me more in my job than anything else. If something doesn't make sense, I keep asking and digging until I find out what is going on. These questions uncover a lot of violations.

Canine Handler: It's tough to single out just one experience but I would have to say playing team sports. While playing team sports I learned communication skills, the importance of physical fitness, team work, being accountable to my team members, following instructions, playing within the rules, commitment to task, etc. In law enforcement, all of these come into play to be successful.

Forensic Artist: The FBI Academy was an amazing learning experience. Now I find that I learn a little more with each case.

Lieutenant: I suppose early on I realized that in order to succeed in life I had to get an education and set goals and make a plan to get me where I wanted to go. I learned from life experience that things would not be handed to me; I would have to earn them. I've learned that success comes from hard work, being responsible and focused, and always following through.

Corrections and Investigative Consultant: There was one single experience I will never forget and that was when I got into some trouble as a youth and realized that I was not cut out for the life of a criminal. The help I received as a juvenile from my Probation Officer helped me when he made me realize I had choices to make in life—that I did not have to accept whatever hand I believed I was dealt. And I believe my experience growing up in a barrio, having to survive the streets, combined with my military experience meeting people from all over the United States and people from other countries in the world where I was stationed while in the military, combined with my later college education while working as a correctional officer or prison guard all helped as well.

Captain: It's hard to describe just one thing that best prepared me for this work. I had a high school teacher who inspired me to continue learning and encouraged me to never close the door on my educational experience—whether it's academic or through life's lessons.

As a dive instructor I attended a program at Dive Rescue International, Inc that provided me with confidence and self-esteem that has carried me very far. As a firefighter and paramedic I have had many close calls and brushes with death that have better prepared me for the next one. I never quit learning and everyday I benefit from another educational experience that better prepares me for work.

Success Lesson #5: **Good choices and hard work are a potent combination.**

- **What are you most proud of in your career?**

Customs and Border Protection Officer: I guess I don't feel I have accomplished any one large, significant achievement. But I am proud of the times that I have kept on when something didn't make sense and ended up uncovering something that led to further investigations. For instance, there was a company trying to smuggle in products that hadn't been approved by the FDA. Another time, someone was trying to smuggle in motorcycles that didn't meet EPA standards. And one time, I turned someone in that ended up being involved in a cocaine-smuggling operation.

Since our authority is only at the borders, we turn these situations over to other kinds of agents to investigate. We don't really get any kind of credit or recognition for what the agents accomplish because of information we've turned over to them. But I am still proud of the times that I was able to sense that there was more going on than what met the eye, and I feel good knowing that the information I turned over to them was valuable in accomplishing a greater goal.

Canine Handler: In 1993 the Louisiana Bankers Association named me the Louisiana Law Enforcement Officer of the Year. In 1998 the Military Order of the World Wars Veterans named me the Law Enforcement Officer of the Year.

Forensic Artist: I am proud of several things. In teaching, I was first runner-up for Law Enforcement Trainer of the Year. One of my students did a composite that identified the largest serial arsonist in the nation. Many of my drawings have helped to identify some pretty nasty people.

Captain: I am most proud of being who I am and doing what I do. I love what I do and the people I serve. I've had some proud moments: delivering babies, saving a building from complete destruction by fire, saving countless lives through advanced life support, recovering family members that have been lost underwater, and being promoted through the ranks. But, most firefighters and paramedics can say the same thing and be just as proud. That's why just being who I am and doing what I do makes me proud.

Lieutenant: My proudest career accomplishment right now is that I ranked number one on my lieutenant's promotional exam.

Corrections and Investigative Consultant: I was appointed as the warden of San Quentin State Prison and served there as warden for 10 years. I took San Quentin from a prison that had been declared "unconstitutional" to "constitutional." The prison was a maximum custody prison with the largest death row in the nation and the largest lock-up maximum units that numbered 1,750 inmates in maximum custody segregation.

Success Lesson #6: **You can learn from other people's mistakes.**

- **Is there anything you wish you had done differently?**

Customs and Border Protection Officer: I wish I had learned earlier not to be so easily intimidated by others—both coworkers and members of the public. Also, I wish that I had trusted my own instincts at times instead of listening to others. Sometimes what is right for someone else isn't necessarily right for me.

Canine Handler: I wish I had graduated from college. Baton Rouge Police Department now offers education pay. I get extra pay for having over 80 hours of college credits. However, if I had a college degree my pay would increase even more.

Lieutenant: If there was anything I would have done differently it would have to be that I would have gone straight to college, received my degree, and then completed a master's degree in law. Of course, it is still not too late. I plan on returning to school soon to complete my bachelor of art's degree.

Corrections and Investigative Consultant: I have no regrets.

Captain: Never give up. Continue your education and pay attention to the little things in life because that's where some of your best life lessons are hidden. Have confidence in yourself and a positive self-esteem, but remain humble. Surround yourself with successful people and avoid trouble.

Life is short, I know that all too well with what I've seen and experienced. Live life, treat people the way you would like to be treated, and learn something new every single day.

Success Lesson #7: A little advice goes a long way.

- **What advice do you have for a young person just getting started?**

  Customs and Border Protection Officer: Get an education in something you really like and take on jobs even if they don't have anything to do with what you eventually want to do. You will be better at any career you choose if you have had a chance to look at things from different perspectives.

  Canine Handler: Treat your profession as a "calling." Stay committed to that calling. You will inevitably face circumstances that aren't pleasing. Do not allow your circumstances to overshadow that calling. It's not always the biggest, brightest, or best that win. If you prepare properly, the most committed will win.

  Forensic Artist: Go to college and learn a variety of skills to make yourself more marketable. Stay away from drugs and stupid decisions—they'll haunt you for the rest of your life and keep you from doing the really fun and fulfilling careers available.

  Lieutenant: My advice to teens is to stay focused on your dreams. You can accomplish anything you set out to do or to become. Stay around positive people. And for the young ladies, I'd say don't allow anyone to influence you in a negative way. Just because you're a women doesn't mean you can't do some of the same things the young men can do.

  Corrections and Investigative Consultant: Set your goals and career objectives and go for them. However, realize that you must prepare yourself first with an education including college graduation. Develop a good reputation with clients for being honest and trustworthy. When you say you're going to do something, do it.

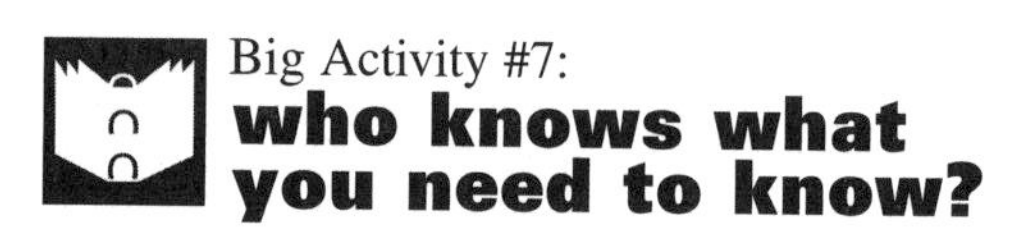

Big Activity #7:

who knows what you need to know?

It's one thing to read about conducting an informational interview, but it's another thing altogether to actually do one. Now it's your turn to shine. Just follow these steps for doing it like a pro!

Step 1: Identify the people you want to talk to about their work.

Step 2: Set up a convenient time to meet in person or talk over the phone.

Step 3: Make up a list of questions that reflect things you'd really like to know about that person's work. Go for the open questions you just read about.

Step 4: Talk away! Take notes as your interviewee responds to each question.

Step 5: Use your notes to write up a "news" article that describes the person and his or her work.

Step 6: Place all your notes and the finished "news" article in your Big Question Answer Book.

Big Activity #7: **who knows what you need to know?**

contact information	appointments/sample questions
name	day time
company	location
title	
address	
	sample questions:
phone	
email	
name	day time
company	location
title	
address	
	sample questions:
phone	
email	
name	day time
company	location
title	
address	
	sample questions:
phone	
email	

CONTACT INFO

Big Activity #7: **who knows what you need to know?**

questions	answers
	INTERVIEW NOTES

Big Activity #7: **who knows what you need to know?**

questions	answers
	INTERVIEW NOTES

Big Activity #7: **who knows what you need to know?**

NEWS

Big Activity #7: **who knows what you need to know?**

NEWS

Big Question #8: how can you find out what a career is really like?

There are some things you just have to figure out for yourself. Things like whether your interest in pursuing a career in marine biology is practical if you plan to live near the Mojave Desert.

Other things you have to see for yourself. Words are sometimes not enough when it comes to conveying what a job is really like on a day-to-day basis—what it looks like, sounds like, and feels like.

Here are a few ideas for conducting an on-the-job reality check.

identify typical types of workplaces

Think of all the places that jobs like the ones you like take place. Almost all of the careers in this book, or ones very similar to them, exist in the corporate world, in the public sector, and in the military. And don't forget the option of going into business for yourself!

For example: Are you interested in public relations? You can find a place for yourself in almost any sector of our economy. Of course, companies definitely want to promote their products. But don't limit yourself to the Fortune 500 corporate world. Hospitals, schools, and manufacturers need your services. Cities, states, and even countries also need your services. They want to increase tourism, get businesses to relocate there, and convince workers to live there or students to study there. Each military branch needs to recruit new members and to show how they are using the money they receive from the government for medical research, taking care of families, and other non-news-breaking uses. Charities, community organizations, and even religious groups want to promote the good things they are doing so that they will get more members, volunteers, contributions, and funding. Political candidates, parties, and special interest groups all want to promote their messages. Even actors, dancers, and writers need to promote themselves.

Not interested in public relations but know you want a career that involves lots of writing? You've thought about becoming the more obvious choices—novelist, newspaper reporter, or English teacher. But you don't want to overlook other interesting possibilities, do you?

What if you also enjoy technical challenges? Someone has to write the documentation for all those computer games and software.

Love cars? Someone has to write those owner's manuals too.

Ditto on those government reports about safety and environmental standards for industries.

Maybe community service is your thing. You can mix your love for helping people with writing grant proposals seeking funds for programs at hospitals, day care centers, or rehab centers.

Talented in art and design? Those graphics you see in magazine advertisements, on your shampoo bottle, and on a box of cereal all have to be created by someone.

That someone could be you.

find out about the job outlook

Organizations like the U.S. Bureau of Labor Statistics spend a lot of time and energy gathering data on what kinds of jobs are most in demand now and what kinds are projected to be in demand in the future. Find out what the job outlook is for a career you like. A good resource for this data can be found on-line at America's Career InfoNet at ***www.acinet.org/acinet.***

This information will help you understand whether the career options you find most appealing are viable. In other words, job outlook data will give you a better sense of your chances of actually finding gainful employment in your chosen profession—a rather important consideration from any standpoint.

Be realistic. You may really, really want to be a film critic at a major newspaper. Maybe your ambition is to become the next Roger Ebert.

Think about this. How many major newspapers are there? Is it reasonable to pin all your career hopes on a job for which there are only about 10 positions in the whole country? That doesn't mean that it's impossible to achieve your ambition. After all, someone has to fill those positions. It should just temper your plans with realism and perhaps encourage you to have a back-up plan, just in case.

look at training requirements

Understand what it takes to prepare yourself for a specific job. Some jobs require only a high school diploma. Others require a couple of years of technical training, while still others require four years or more in college.

Be sure to investigate a variety of training options. Look at training programs and colleges you may like to attend. Check out their websites to see what courses are required for the major you want. Make sure you're willing to "do the time" in school to prepare yourself for a particular occupation.

see for yourself

There's nothing quite like seeing for yourself what a job is like. Talk with a teacher or guidance counselor to arrange a job-shadowing opportunity with someone who is in the job or in a similar one.

Job shadowing is an activity that involves actually spending time at work with someone to see what a particular job is like up close and personal. It's an increasingly popular option and your school may participate in specially designated job-shadowing days. For some especially informative resources on job shadowing, visit ***www.jobshadow.org***.

Another way to test-drive different careers is to find summer jobs and internships that are similar to the career you hope to pursue.

make a Plan B

Think of the alternatives! Often it's not possible to have a full-time job in the field you love. Some jobs just don't pay enough to meet the needs of every person or family. Maybe you recognize that you don't have the talent, drive, or commitment to rise to the top. Or, perhaps you can't afford the years of work it takes to get established or you place a higher priority on spending time with family than that career might allow.

If you can see yourself in any of those categories, DO NOT GIVE UP on what you love! There is always more than one way to live out your dreams. Look at some of the other possibilities in this book. Find a way to integrate your passion into other jobs or your free time.

Lots of people manage to accomplish this in some fairly impressive ways. For instance, the Knicks City Dancers, known for their incredible performances and for pumping up the crowd at Knicks basketball games, include an environmental engineer, a TV news assignment editor, and a premed student, in addition to professional dancers. The Broadband Pickers, a North Texas bluegrass band, is made up of five lawyers and one businessman. In fact, even people who are extremely successful in a field that they love find ways to indulge their other passions. Paul Newman, the actor and director, not only drives race cars as a hobby, but also produces a line of gourmet foods and donates the profits to charity.

Get the picture? Good. Hang in there and keep moving forward in your quest to find your way toward a great future.

Big Activity #8:

how can you find out what a career is really like?

This activity will help you conduct a reality check about your future career in two ways. First, it prompts you to find out more about the nitty-gritty details you really need to know to make a well-informed career choice. Second, it helps you identify strategies for getting a firsthand look at what it's like to work in a given profession—day in and day out.

Here's how to get started:

Step 1: Write the name of the career you're considering at the top of a sheet of paper (or use the following worksheets if this is your book).

Step 2: Create a checklist (or, if this is your book, use the one provided on the following pages) covering two types of reality-check items.

First, list four types of information to investigate:

- training requirements
- typical workplaces
- job outlook
- similar occupations

Second, list three types of opportunities to pursue:

- job shadowing
- apprenticeship
- internship

Step 3: Use resources such as America's Career InfoNet at ***www.acinet.org*** and Career OneStop at ***www.careeronestop.org*** to seek out the information you need.

Step 4: Make an appointment with your school guidance counselor to discuss how to pursue hands-on opportunities to learn more about this occupation. Use the space provided on the following worksheets to jot down preliminary contact information and a brief summary of why or why not each career is right for you.

Step 5: When you're finished, place these notes in your Big Question AnswerBook.

Big Activity #8: **how can you find out what a career is really like?**

career choice:	
training requirements	
typical workplaces	
job outlook	
similar occupations	

INFORMATION

Big Activity #8: **how can you find out what a career is really like?**

job shadowing	when: where: who: observations and impressions:
apprenticeship	when: where: who: observations and impressions:
internship	when: where: who: observations and impressions:

OPPORTUNITIES

Big Question #9: how do you know when you've made the right choice?

When it comes right down to it, finding the career that's right for you is like shopping in a mall with 12,000 different stores. Finding the right fit may require trying on lots of different options.

All the Big Questions you've answered so far have been designed to expand your career horizons and help you clarify what you really want in a career. The next step is to see how well you've managed to integrate your interests, capabilities, goals, and ambitions with the realities of specific opportunities.

There are two things for you to keep in mind as you do this.

First, recognize the value of all the hard work you did to get to this point. If you've already completed the first eight activities thoughtfully and honestly, whatever choices you make will be based on solid knowledge about yourself and your options. You've learned to use a process that works just as well now, when you're trying to get an inkling of what you want to do with your life, as it will later when you have solid job offers on the table and need to make decisions that will affect your life and family.

Second, always remember that sometimes, even when you do everything right, things don't turn out the way you'd planned. That's called life. It happens. And it's not the end of the world. Even if you make what seems to be a bad choice, know this—there's no such thing as a wasted experience. The paths you take, the training you receive, the people you meet—they ultimately fall together like puzzle pieces to make you who you are and prepare you for what you're meant to do.

That said, here's a strategy to help you confirm that you are making the very best choices you can.

Big Activity #9:

how do you know when you've made the right choice?

One way to confirm that the choices you are making are right for you is to look at both sides of this proverbial coin: what you are looking for and what each career offers. The following activity will help you think this through.

Step 1: To get started, make two charts with four columns (or, if this is your book, use the following worksheets).

Step 2: Label the first column of the first chart as "Yes Please!" Under this heading list all the qualities you absolutely must have in a future job. This might include factors such as the kind of training you'd prefer to pursue (college, apprenticeship, etc.); the type of place where you'd like to work (big office, high-tech lab, in the great outdoors, etc.); and the sorts of people you want to work with (children, adults, people with certain needs, etc.). It may also include salary requirements or dress code preferences.

Step 3: Now at the top of the next three columns write the names of three careers you are considering. (This is a little like Big Activity #3 where you examined your work values. But now you know a lot more and you're ready to zero in on specific careers.)

Step 4: Go down the list and use an *X* to indicate careers that do indeed feature the desired preferences. Use an *O* to indicate those that do not.

Step 5: Tally up the number of *Xs* and *Os* at the bottom of each career column to find out which comes closest to your ideal job.

Step 6: In the first column of the second chart add a heading called "No Thanks!" This is where you'll record the factors you simply prefer not to deal with. Maybe long hours, physically demanding work, or jobs that require years of advanced training just don't cut it for you. Remember that part of figuring out what you do want to do involves understanding what you don't want to do.

Step 7: Repeat steps 2 through 5 for these avoid-at-all-costs preferences as you did for the must-have preferences above.

Big Activity #9: **how do you know when you've made the right choice?**

yes please!	career #1	career #2	career #3
totals	__X__O	__X__O	__X__O

Big Activity #9: **how do you know when you've made the right choice?**

no thanks!	career #1	career #2	career #3
totals	___X___O	___X___O	___X___O

Big Question #10: what's next?

Think of this experience as time well invested in your future. And expect it to pay off in a big way down the road. By now, you have worked (and perhaps wrestled) your way through nine important questions:

- Big Question #1: **who are you?**
- Big Question #2: **what are your interests and strengths?**
- Big Question #3: **what are your work values?**
- Big Question #4: **what is your work personality?**
- Big Question #5: **do you have the right skills?**
- Big Question #6: **are you on the right path?**
- Big Question #7: **who knows what you need to know?**
- Big Question #8: **how can you find out what a career is really like?**
- Big Question #9: **how do you know when you've made the right choice?**

But what if you still don't have a clue about what you want to do with your life?

Don't worry. You're talking about one of the biggest life decisions you'll ever make. These things take time.

It's okay if you don't have all the definitive answers yet. At least you do know how to go about finding them. The process you've used to work through this book is one that you can rely on throughout your life to help you sort through the options and make sound career decisions.

So what's next?

More discoveries, more exploration, and more experimenting with success are what come next. Keep at it and you're sure to find your way to wherever your dreams and ambitions lead you.

And, just for good measure, here's one more Big Activity to help point you in the right direction.

Big Activity #10: **what's next?**

List five things you can do to move forward in your career planning process (use a separate sheet if you need to). Your list may include tasks such as talking to your guidance counselor about resources your school makes available, checking out colleges or other types of training programs that can prepare you for your life's work, or finding out about job-shadowing or internship opportunities in your community. Remember to include any appropriate suggestions from the Get Started Now! list included with each career profile in Section 2 of this book.

Big Activity #10: **what's next?**

career planning to-do list
1
2
3
4
5

a final word

You are now officially equipped with the tools you need to track down a personally appropriate profession any time you have the need or desire. You've discovered more about who you are and what you want. You've explored a variety of career options within a very important industry. You've even taken it upon yourself to experiment with what it might be like to actually work in certain occupations.

Now it's up to you to put all this newfound knowledge to work for you. While you're at it, here's one more thing to keep in mind: Always remember that there's no such thing as a wasted experience. Certainly some experiences are more positive than others, but they all teach us something.

Chances are you may not get everything right the first time out. It may turn out that you were incorrect about how much you would love to go to a certain college or pursue a particular profession. That doesn't mean you're doomed to failure. It simply means that you've lived and learned. Sometimes you just won't know for sure about one direction or another until you try things out a bit. Nothing about your future has to be written in stone. Allow yourself some freedom to experiment with various options until you find something that really clicks for you.

Figuring out what you want to do with the rest of your life is a big deal. It's probably one of the most exciting and among the most intimidating decisions you'll ever make. It's a decision that warrants clearheaded thought and wholehearted investigation. It's a process that's likely to take you places you never dared imagine if you open yourself up to all the possibilities. Take a chance on yourself and seek out and follow your most valued hopes and dreams into the workplace.

Best wishes for a bright future!

Appendix

a virtual support team

As you continue your quest to determine just what it is you want to do with your life, you'll find that you are not alone. There are many people and organizations who want to help you succeed. Here are two words of advice—let them! Take advantage of all the wonderful resources so readily available to you.

The first place to start is your school's guidance center. There you are quite likely to find a variety of free resources which include information about careers, colleges, and other types of training opportunities; details about interesting events, job shadowing activities, and internship options; and access to useful career assessment tools.

In addition, since you are the very first generation on the face of the earth to have access to a world of information just the click of a mouse away—use it! The following Internet resources provide all kinds of information and ideas that can help you find your future.

make an informed choice

Following are five of the very best career-oriented websites currently on-line. Be sure to bookmark these websites and visit them often as you consider various career options.

America's Career InfoNet ***www.acinet.org/acinet/default.asp***

Quite possibly the most comprehensive source of career exploration anywhere, this U.S. Department of Labor website includes all kinds of current information about wages, market conditions, employers, and employment trends. Make sure to visit the site's career video library where you'll find links to over 450 videos featuring real people doing real jobs.

Careers & Colleges ***www.careersandcolleges.com***

Each year Careers & Colleges publishes four editions of *Careers & Colleges* magazine, designed to help high school students set and meet their academic, career, and financial goals. Ask your guidance counselor about receiving free copies. You'll also want to visit the excellent Careers and Colleges website. Here you'll encounter their "Virtual Guidance Counselor," an interactive career database that allows you to match your interests with college majors or careers that are right for you.

Career Voyages ***www.careervoyages.gov***

This website is brought to you compliments of collaboration between the U.S. Department of Labor and the U.S. Department of Education and is designed especially for students like you. Here you'll find information on high-growth, high-demand occupations and the skills and education needed to attain those jobs.

Job Shadow *www.jobshadow.org*
See your future via a variety of on-line virtual job-shadowing videos and interviews featuring people with fascinating jobs.

My Cool Career *www.mycoolcareer.com*
This website touts itself as the "coolest career dream site for teens and 20's." See for yourself as you work your way through a variety of useful self-assessment quizzes, listen to an assortment of on-line career shows, and explore all kinds of career resources.

investigate local opportunities

To get a better understanding of employment happenings in your state, visit these state-specific career information websites.

Alabama
www.ajb.org/al
www.al.plusjobs.com

Alaska
www.jobs.state.ak.us
www.akcis.org/default.htm

Arizona
www.ajb.org/az
www.ade.state.az.us/cte/AZCrn project10.asp

Arkansas
www.ajb.org/ar
www.careerwatch.org
www.ioscar.org/ar

California
www.calmis.ca.gov
www.ajb.org/ca
www.eurekanet.org

Colorado
www.coloradocareer.net
www.coworkforce.com/lmi

Connecticut
www1.ctdol.state.ct.us/jcc
www.ctdol.state.ct.us/lmi

Delaware
www.ajb.org/de
www.delewareworks.com

District of Columbia
www.ajb.org/dc
www.dcnetworks.org

Florida
www.Florida.access.bridges.com
www.employflorida.net

Georgia
www.gcic.peachnet.edu
(Ask your school guidance counselor for your school's free password and access code)
www.dol.state.ga.us/js

Hawaii
www.ajb.org/hi
www.careerkokua.org

Idaho
www.ajb.org/id
www.cis.idaho.gov

Illinois
www.ajb.org/il
www.ilworkinfo.com

Indiana
www.ajb.org/in
http://icpac.indiana.edu

Iowa
www.ajb.org/ia
www.state.ia.us/iccor

Kansas
www.ajb.org/ks
www.kansasjoblink.com/ada

Kentucky
www.ajb.org/ky

Louisiana
www.ajb.org/la
www.ldol.state.la.us/jobpage.asp

Maine
www.ajb.org/me
www.maine.gov/labor/lmis

Maryland
www.ajb.org/md
www.careernet.state.md.us

Massachusetts
www.ajb.org/ma
http://masscis.intocareers.org

Michigan
www.mois.org

Minnesota
www.ajb.org/mn
www.iseek.org

Mississippi
www.ajb.org/ms
www.mscareernet.org

Missouri
www.ajb.org/mo
www.greathires.org

Montana
www.ajb.org/mt
http://jsd.dli.state.mt.us/mjshome.asp

Nebraska
www.ajb.org/ne
www.careerlink.org

New Hampshire
www.nhes.state.nh.us

New Jersey
www.ajb.org/nj
www.wnjpin.net/coei

New Mexico
www.ajb.org/nm
www.dol.state.nm.us/soicc/upto21.html

Nevada
www.ajb.org/nv
http://nvcis.intocareers.org

New York
www.ajb.org/ny
www.nycareerzone.org

North Carolina
www.ajb.org/nc
www.ncsoicc.org
www.nccareers.org

North Dakota
www.ajb.org/nd
www.imaginend.com
www.ndcrn.com/students

Ohio
www.ajb.org/oh
https://scoti.ohio.gov/scoti_lexs

Oklahoma
www.ajb.org/ok
www.okcareertech.org/guidance
http://okcrn.org

Oregon
www.hsd.k12.or.us/crls

Pennsylvania
www.ajb.org/pa
www.pacareerlink.state.pa.us

Rhode Island
www.ajb.org/ri
www.dlt.ri.gov/lmi/jobseeker.htm

South Carolina
www.ajb.org/sc
www.scois.org/students.htm

South Dakota
www.ajb.org/sd

Tennessee
www.ajb.org/tn
www.tcids.utk.edu

Texas
www.ajb.org/tx
www.ioscar.org/tx
www.cdr.state.tx.us/Hotline/Hotline.html

Utah
www.ajb.org/ut
http://jobs.utah.gov/wi/occi.asp

Vermont
www.ajb.org/vt
www.vermontjoblink.com
www.vtlmi.info/oic.cfm

Virginia
www.ajb.org/va
www.vacrn.net

Washington
www.ajb.org/wa
www.workforceexplorer.com
www.wa.gov/esd/lmea/soicc/sohome.htm

West Virginia
www.ajb.org/wv
www.state.wv.us/bep/lmi

Wisconsin
www.ajb.org/wi
www.careers4wi.wisc.edu
http://wiscareers.wisc.edu/splash.asp

Wyoming
www.ajb.org/wy
http://uwadmnweb.uwyo.edu/SEO/wcis.htm

get a job

Whether you're curious about the kinds of jobs currently in big demand or you're actually looking for a job, the following websites are a great place to do some virtual job-hunting.

America's Job Bank *www.ajb.org*
Another example of your (or, more accurately, your parent's) tax dollars at work, this well-organized website is sponsored by the U.S. Department of Labor. Job seekers can post resumes and use the site's search engines to search through over a million job listings by location or by job type.

Monster.com *www.monster.com*
One of the Internet's most widely used employment websites, this is where you can search for specific types of jobs in specific parts of the country, network with millions of people, and find useful career advice.

explore by special interests

An especially effective way to explore career options is to look at careers associated with a personal interest or fascination with a certain type of industry. The following websites help you narrow down your options in a focused way.

What Interests You? *www.bls.gov/k12*
This Bureau of Labor Statistics website provides information about careers associated with 12 special interest areas: math, reading, science, social studies, music and arts, building and fixing things, helping people, computers, law, managing money, sports, and nature.

Construct My Future *www.constructmyfuture.com*
With over $600 billion annually devoted to new construction projects, about 6 million Americans build careers in this industry. This website, sponsored by the Association of Equipment Distributors, the Association of Equipment Manufacturers, and Associated General Contractors, introduces an interesting array of construction-related professions.

Dream It Do It *www.dreamit-doit.com*
In order to make manufacturing a preferred career choice by 2010, the National Association of Manufacturing's Center for Workforce Success is reaching out to young adults and, their parents, educators, communities, and policy-makers to change their minds about manufacturing's future and its careers. This website introduces high-demand 21st-century manufacturing professions many will find surprising and worthy of serious consideration.

Get Tech *www.gettech.org*
Another award-winning website from the National Association of Manufacturing.

Take Another Look *www.Nrf.com/content/foundation/rcp/main.htm*
The National Retail Federation challenges students to take another look at their industry by introducing a wide variety of careers associated with marketing and advertising, store management, sales, distribution and logistics, e-commerce, and more.

Index

Page numbers in **boldface** indicate main articles. Page numbers in *italics* indicate photographs.

C

D

E

F

M

N

O

T

U

V

W

Y